BECOMING AN UNSTOPPABLE WOMAN

ADRIANA LUNA CARLOS
Editor-In-Chief, Designer and Co-Founder

HANNA OLIVAS
Managing Editor & Co-Founder

ADVERTISING OPPORTUNITIES

Info@SheRisesStudios.com

BAUW MAGAZINE
DECEMBER 2025

SHE RISES STUDIOS

CONTACT US

editorial@sherisesstudios.com

WWW.SHERISESSTUDIOS.COM

LETTER FROM THE EDITORS

Dear Readers,

As we close out 2025, we find ourselves returning to a truth that women across every generation have always carried: real power comes from within. This December, Becoming an Unstoppable Woman Magazine honors that truth through our theme, Reflection and Renewal: The Power Within, a celebration of the inner strength, emotional courage, and transformational generosity that define unstoppable women.

This edition, Women Empowering Change Through Giving, highlights the women who not only rise for themselves but rise for others. Their impact is not measured in titles or accolades, but in the lives they touch, the communities they lift, and the legacies they leave behind. Through giving, mentoring, leading, and loving boldly, these women remind us that empowerment is not simply an action; it is a ripple that expands across generations.

Our December cover feature, Aura Elena Martinez, embodies that ripple effect with remarkable clarity. Her work in self-discovery, emotional education, and empowerment has helped women around the world reconnect with who they truly are. Aura's message echoes the heartbeat of this edition: that fulfillment begins within, purpose reveals itself through inner alignment, and the greatest transformation comes from returning home to ourselves.

Inside these pages, you will meet women who have turned their personal healing into global impact, who choose generosity even when life demands strength, and who lead with vision rooted in self-awareness. Their stories invite all of us to pause, reflect, and renew the commitments we make to our growth, our wellbeing, and the change we want to see in the world.

As we step into a new year, may this edition inspire you to embrace your own reflection, trust your inner wisdom, and allow your renewal to become a gift not only to yourself, but to the world around you.

With admiration for your journey and your power within,

Adriana Luna Carlos, Hanna Olivas
Editors of BAUW Magazine

Become a Managing Partner

she wins
WOMEN'S NETWORK

Join a global Movement of Visionary Women
50+ Chapters. Transformative Community. Unlimited Growth.

WHAT'S INCLUDED

- 40% commission on memberships + event bonuses
- Leadership training, toolkits & ongoing support
- VIP access to retreats, masterminds & more

Join for just

www.shewinswomensnetwork.com

Application Fee (paid only after acceptance)

Becoming An Unstoppable Woman Magazine

AWAKENING THE SELF:

HOW AURA ELENA MARTINEZ HELPS WOMEN LIVE WITH CLARITY, PURPOSE, AND FULFILLMENT

By **She Rises Studios Editorial Team**

For Aura E. Martinez, the journey of empowerment begins where most people rarely look: within. As a Self-Discovery and Empowerment Coach and the creator of the Aura Blueprint™, she has dedicated her life to helping women gain clarity in their purpose and wake up each day feeling fulfilled, certain, and fully alive. Through her coaching, books, and global influence, Aura reminds women that the most extraordinary journey they will ever take is not across continents but into the depths of their own being.

Her own path to this work has been as expansive as it has been transformative. As a Flight Attendant, Aura traveled across the world, witnessing the vast diversity of human culture and lifestyle. Yet among all the destinations she visited, one revelation stood out above the rest. The most remarkable place anyone can explore is themselves.

Becoming An Unstoppable Woman Magazine

"We do not think twice about seeing the good, bad, and the uncomfortable parts of other countries," she reflects. "But what about ourselves? Every part of us holds jewels that would amaze us if we only took the time to look and learn." This understanding became the heart of her mission: to guide women back to their essence so they can create lives rooted in authenticity and inner truth.

At the center of her work is the Aura Blueprint™, a four-part framework designed to lead women from confusion to clarity. Each letter in her name represents a key stage of the journey. First is Assess, which helps women identify where they are and where they want to go. Next is Understand, where they uncover the fears, patterns, and limiting beliefs that have kept them stuck. Then comes Realign, the process of reconnecting with their true identity. The final stage is Aliveness, when their inner world begins to match their outer world. *"These steps are essential for the daily fulfillment women seek,"* Aura explains. *"The blueprint frees them from the stories and pain they have been carrying so they can finally live from authenticity."*

Her philosophy of teaching women to wake up to a life of fulfillment did not emerge by accident. It grew from observing the inner barriers that hold so many women back. She identifies three major blocks: the fear of facing oneself, unconscious patterns that drive behavior, and the tendency to avoid inner work. *"Many women are afraid of what they will discover if they slow down long enough to listen,"* she says.

"But meeting your own truth is where clarity begins." She adds that unconscious beliefs shape choices more than people realize. Without awareness of what lives beneath the surface, many continue living on autopilot. The third block, avoiding inner work, shows up when people chase external solutions rather than deeper self-connection. *"Transformation happens when you turn inward. That is where everything begins to make sense."*

Her global travels also shaped her understanding of well-being. Moving through different cultures gave her a firsthand look at how environments influence self-perception. *"Culture affects how we think, behave, and feel,"* she shares. *"If your environment praises a certain body type or personality, it can influence your view of yourself. When you learn to distinguish what belongs to you from what belongs to the world around you, you protect your well-being."* This insight strengthened her belief that self-discovery is essential for emotional and mental freedom.

This same philosophy inspired her movement, Live to the Max™ and Viva al máximo™, which encourages individuals to live fully and authentically. *"Living to the max means living according to who you really are,"* Aura explains. *"It is choosing from truth, not fear. It is waking up with purpose and going to bed with peace, knowing you showed up as yourself."* For her, living to the max is not about chasing perfection or constant happiness. It is about embracing wholeness and living without the inner restrictions that once held you back.

Her bestselling book, Creating a Lifetime of Wellness, and its companion journal expand on this idea of personalized transformation. The core message she hopes readers take with them is the importance of self-discovery in every area of life. *"We are all different. What works for one person may not work for another. When you know yourself, you know how to create change that fits who you are."*

Aura recognizes a distinct moment that signals when a woman is stepping into her true path. It is the moment she stops looking outward for answers and begins trusting her own voice. *"There is a quiet shift,"* she explains. *"She realizes she already knows what she needs. She stops forcing what does not fit and begins choosing what aligns."* This is where clarity begins to flow naturally because she is no longer betraying herself to meet expectations.

To help women reconnect with their inner truth, Aura encourages simple daily practices. Journaling helps release mental noise and brings clarity to emotions and decisions. Meditation, even in quiet moments with a morning cup of coffee, creates space to observe thoughts without judgment. Morning check-ins help identify what is needed emotionally or mentally before the day begins. These practices may seem small, but they strengthen self-awareness, which Aura considers the foundation of empowerment.

When someone feels overwhelmed by the idea of finding their purpose, Aura shifts their focus away from trying to figure it out and toward reconnecting with themselves. *"Purpose is not something you chase,"* she says. *"It emerges naturally when you come home to yourself. When you understand who you are, your purpose begins to reveal itself."*

Looking into the future, Aura sees the Aura Blueprint™ and Live to the Max™ evolving into global movements that equip women with emotional education and self-awareness tools.

"I want every woman to have access to the language and practices that help her understand herself and trust her intuition," she shares. Her vision includes programs, retreats, books, and digital platforms that support women across generations. *"When one woman awakens to her power, she changes the lineage that comes after her."*

For Aura E. Martinez, self-discovery is not a luxury. It is the gateway to fulfillment, clarity, and real freedom. Through her work, she continues to remind women that purpose is not found in the world around them. It is uncovered within. And when a woman finally sees herself clearly, she unlocks a level of alignment and aliveness that changes everything. Because the most extraordinary place she will ever explore is the one she carries within her.

Connect With Aura

www.instagram.com/AuraElenaMartinez;
www.facebook.com/AuraEMartinezCoach
www.tiktok.com/@auraemartinez
www.youtube.com/@AuraEMartinez
www.linkedin.com/in/aura-elena-martinez

Get Your Free Playbook:
How to Attract Your Soul Tribe ...
Magically!

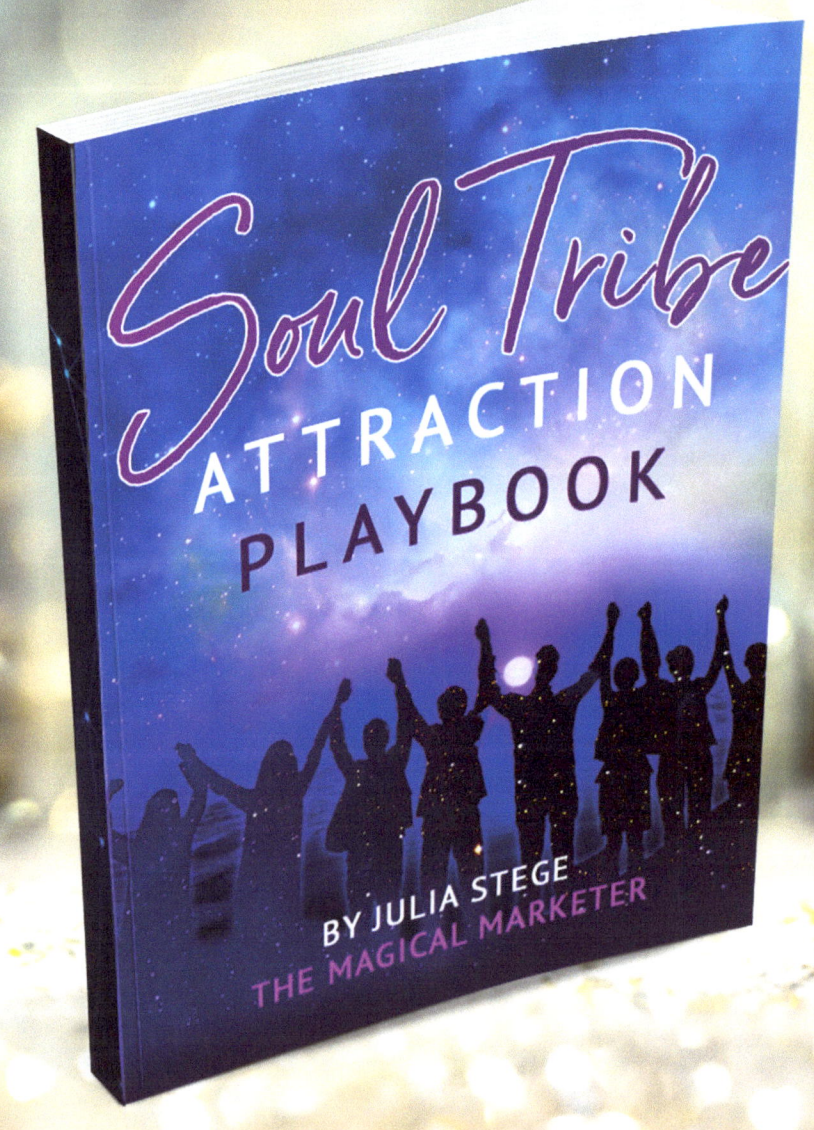

Empower your marketing with ancient mystical laws.
Attract divinely aligned clients by following your Soul.
MagicalPlaybook.com

CALL FOR AUTHORS

ONBOARDING VOLUMES 2 & 3 OF THE GIRL ON THE LEFT

APPLY NOW

BEFORE & AFTER WOMEN'S STORIES
SPRING / FALL 2026 RELEASES

CONTACT: HELLO@THEGIRLONTHELEFT.COM
PUBLISHED IN PARTNERSHIP WITH SHE RISES STUDIOS

Becoming An Unstoppable Magazine

© THE NEW YORK FAMILY OFFICE CONFERENCE

FASHIONING CHANGE:

LAUREN BUSH AND THE POWER OF PURPOSE-DRIVEN RENEWAL

Becoming An Unstoppable Woman Magazine

By **She Rises Studios Editorial Team**

As the year draws to a close and we collectively turn inward to reflect on growth, change, and renewal, few stories embody the spirit of transformation more profoundly than that of **Lauren Bush**, founder of **FEED Projects**. From fashion model and designer to social entrepreneur and humanitarian, Lauren's journey reflects what happens when style meets substance—and when reflection fuels purposeful action.

Born into a world that could have easily defined her by name or lineage, Lauren Bush refused to let privilege dictate her story. Instead, she chose to leverage her platform for impact. In 2007, inspired by her travels as an honorary student ambassador with the United Nations World Food Programme, Lauren founded **FEED Projects**—a social enterprise built on a simple yet powerful idea: that every consumer purchase can contribute to ending world hunger.

FEED's iconic burlap bags—each stamped with a number representing the meals provided through its sale—are more than just fashion statements. They are emblems of compassion, empowerment, and sustainable progress. Through these products, FEED has provided over **120 million meals** to children and families worldwide. But beyond the numbers, the brand tells a deeper story of reflection and renewal—of how one person's decision to act can ripple outward and transform lives across the globe.

For Lauren, **renewal isn't about reinvention for the sake of change—it's about returning to what truly matters.** *"The more I learned about hunger and inequality, the more I realized how interconnected we all are,"* she once shared. *"FEED became my way of channeling reflection into action—of making giving tangible."* Her mission perfectly mirrors the essence of this season: looking back with gratitude, acknowledging the lessons learned, and stepping forward with greater clarity and purpose.

The power of **reflection** in Lauren's story lies in her ability to see fashion not as a vehicle for vanity, but as a tool for visibility. By blending conscious design with global impact, she reshaped what it means to be both creative and compassionate in business. Every bag, accessory, and collaboration she launches tells a story of women artisans—from Guatemala to Kenya—whose craftsmanship not only sustains their families but also redefines empowerment in their communities.

This approach embodies **renewal at its most meaningful**: the act of using one's platform to uplift others while reimagining an industry. In a world where fast fashion dominates and consumption often overshadows conscience, Lauren stands as a reminder that change begins with intention. Her leadership invites women everywhere to consider how their choices—both personal and professional—can serve as catalysts for good.

As we close out the year, Lauren's example encourages us all to pause and ask: *What am I creating with my time, my voice, my resources?* The answers may not come all at once, but reflection offers the clarity to align with our deeper purpose. Renewal, after all, isn't about starting over—it's about moving forward with wisdom, gratitude, and a heart anchored in service.

Through FEED, Lauren Bush continues to turn a simple concept into a global movement of mindful giving. Her story is a testament to the idea that real power doesn't come from recognition or success—it comes from courage, empathy, and the willingness to act.

In honoring women like Lauren, we celebrate not just their achievements but the **power within** that drives them to create lasting change. As this season of reflection unfolds, may we each find inspiration to renew our sense of purpose—to look back with pride, give thanks for the lessons learned, and step boldly into a new year ready to make a difference.

Because when reflection meets action, renewal becomes unstoppable—and so do we.

www.sherisesstudios.com

DON'T DRIFT INTO THE NEXT YEAR:

HOW TO BUILD A 2026 PLAN THAT INSPIRES ACTION, ACCOUNTABILITY, AND OWNERSHIP

By **Meryl Simmons**

Every year I watch it happen:

CEO hits Q4 and says, *"We need a plan for next year."*
Then a familiar cycle begins:
- A planning meeting is booked.
- A slide deck is created.
- The plan gets filed away and is never seen again.

By February, the business is back in reaction mode - putting out fires and basically drifting through.

It's not that the plan failed.

It's that there was *no system* to execute it.

Why traditional planning fails

Traditional annual planning feels good in the moment. It's exciting to brainstorm goals, dream big, and envision growth. But here's why most plans fall apart before they generate results:

1. The vision stays in the leader's head
The team hears it once, then goes back to business as usual.

2. There are too many goals
When everything is important, nothing is important.
3. There's no accountability rhythm
If you don't keep score, you can't win.
4. The plan lives in a 20-page deck no one revisits
Strategy without execution is just wishful thinking.

Businesses don't struggle because they lack ideas. They struggle because they lack clarity, focus, and follow-through.

How to break through: Purpose-based planning

Creating a meaningful 2026 plan starts with a shift:
"People don't commit to goals...they commit to what they helped create."

Your job as a leader isn't just to set the direction. It's to help your team *own it.*

Purpose-based planning gives every team member ownership of:
- Daily activity
- Quarterly priorities
- Annual goals
- The long-term vision

With this approach, 2026 becomes something your team is *building*, not another event.

The framework: Vision → Traction → Accountability

To build a 2026 plan that inspires execution, not just excitement, you only need three components:

1. Vision: Define the destination

Most companies operate below potential because don't actually lack clarity. They lack *documented* clarity. Once your vision is written down, it becomes repeatable.

Use a simple, 2-page tool (like the Vision/Traction Organizer®) to answer:
- Where are we going?
- What does success look like?
- What must we say *no* to?

2. Traction: Make the vision move

Break the annual goals into quarterly priorities, called Rocks.

Three rules:
- Fewer is better
- Each Rock must have one owner
- Every Rock must be measurable

Because if everyone owns a goal... **no one owns it.**

3. Accountability: Keep the plan alive

A Weekly Scorecard™ is a document (like this below) with 5 - 15 leading indicators that keeps progress visible.

Not monthly.
Not quarterly.
Weekly.

You need this in your business because monthly reporting tells you what already happened and weekly reporting tells you what's *about to happen.* Here a little video I made showing how to create this for yourself

A real example

A consulting firm I worked with used to start each year energized...until Q2 came and no one could remember what the annual goals were.

We implemented the Vision/Traction Organizer®, set quarterly Rocks, and introduced a Weekly Scorecard™.

In 90 days:
- The team was aligned
- Accountability improved
- Revenue increased because everyone knew exactly what to execute

Nothing changed about their talent. Everything changed about their **focus** and **discipline.**

You can choose to drift into 2026, or you can design it.

A plan on 20 slides is a presentation and a plan broken into weekly actions is **inevitable progress.**

I've put together a free **2026 Vision-to-Execution Clarity Kit** to help you get started. You'll get the exact 2-page planning tool I use with clients in full-day, $6,000 strategy sessions free. Work your way through the kit, and you'll be rewarded with a completed plan for 2026...clarity, priorities, and accountability included.

Here's to a profitable, well-executed 2026!

Connect With Meryl

www.claritycoach.io
www.linkedin.com/in/merylsimmons

RESILIENCE THROUGH REINVENTION:
RISING FROM THE ASHES OF CHANGE

By **Brenda "Bre" Bardaels, PsyD (c)**

Every January, I start with intention. As a doctoral researcher, Army National Guard officer, and woman determined to grow with purpose, I began 2025 with one clear goal: finish and defend my dissertation proposal. I had spent months studying leadership and psychological safety to understand how people rebuild trust after adversity. What I didn't know was that my year would become a living experiment in resilience itself.

In early January, the Palisades fires broke out across California, and my plans were instantly transformed. Overnight, I traded academic writing for field gear, answering the call to serve as part of the California Army National Guard's response team. For weeks, our mission was to provide relief, structure, and safety amid chaos. Flames consumed not only homes but dreams, plans, and a sense of normalcy. Families were displaced; communities were shattered.

Amid the ashes, I learned what it truly means to pivot with purpose.

Reinvention Is Not Failure. It's Evolution

In my book Not Your Average Leader, I wrote that leadership begins where comfort ends. Reinvention, like leadership, demands surrender, letting go of what we thought life should look like so we can discover what it can become.

During the fires, I learned that resilience isn't about *"bouncing back."* It's about building forward. I carved out moments in my tent to revise my dissertation proposal by flashlight. Some nights, I wrote while exhaustion blurred the words. Other nights, I reminded myself that persistence is its own form of healing. When I finally got to come home and defended my proposal successfully, it was an academic milestone and a declaration of survival.

The truth is reinvention often begins when our old plans no longer fit the person we are becoming. For many of us women balancing careers, families, studies, or service, this past year demanded a courage we didn't know we had. Some lost homes or jobs; others faced burnout or transitions that forced them to redefine success. I see these women not as broken but as reborn, reshaped by fire, refined by purpose.

Reflection as a Tool for Renewal

Resilience requires reflection. During quiet moments after deactivation, I began journaling, something I encourage every woman to do.

Reflection turns experience into wisdom. It helps us see patterns, name our growth, and forgive ourselves for what didn't go as planned.

Ask yourself: What did this season teach me? What must I release to move forward?

The answers may surprise you. Sometimes the greatest renewal comes not from adding more to your life, but from releasing what no longer serves your peace.

The Power Within

When the fires died down, many of us began rebuilding, not just homes, but identities. I returned to my research with deeper empathy and purpose. My dissertation, which explores how destructive leadership impacts psychological safety, now feels more urgent than ever. Because resilience isn't built in isolation; it grows in the spaces where leaders nurture trust, compassion, and inclusion.

For every woman closing out 2025 feeling weary, uncertain, or stretched thin, remember this: renewal is not a luxury, it's a necessity. Reinvention is not the end of your story; it's the rewriting of its draft.

Sometimes life's fires don't destroy us, they illuminate the path to who we were meant to become.

Connect With Bre

www.notyouraverageleaderbook.com
Instagram: @Bre_At_Losal

Becoming An Unstoppable Woman Magazine

Live Your 2026 Purpose

Discover Your Radiant Awakening

Feeling blocked or drained? Like you're meant for something more? **This is your moment! Start 2026 with purpose.**

"I was in a major life transition. Katia helped me grow tremendously and connect deeply with myself, and I don't think my life would be where it is without our time together!" -Lexie

Awaken your purpose and release what's holding you back. **Radiant Awakening** guides women to uncover fulfilling work that lights up their lives, through personalized guidance and chakra-focused healing. **Gain clarity, confidence, & actionable steps** to create a career and life that excites you.

Book a call today to explore what's truly possible for your career and purpose: **innerrainbowhealing.com**

Our hybrid group/individual program starts **January 6th. Limited spots available**-- let's make 2026 your year of transformation!

REFLECTION AND RENEWAL:
THE POWER WITHIN

By **Julie Colombino-Billingham**
Author and Founder of Deux Mains

My own path began in the aftermath of Haiti's 2010 earthquake. I arrived as a disaster response volunteer, hoping to help rebuild a country that was ravaged by disaster. What I found instead, was a community of women determined to rebuild what the earthquake destroyed. Despite immense loss, their courage was contagious and they changed my life. I was inspired to create something that could outlast the tragedy all around us, and we built a fashion business with independence and sustainability at the forefront.

That vision became Deux Mains, a fair-trade fashion brand handcrafting beautiful leather bags and goods in Haiti. Over time, we weathered political instability, natural disasters, and global supply chain disruptions. Each challenge taught us something vital, that reflection isn't passive; it's the birthplace of transformation.

Reflection: The Quiet Force Behind Resilience

Allowing for reflection can often be mistaken for pause, but in truth, it's motion in another form. It's the process that allows us to make sense of disruption, to extract meaning from hardship, and to chart a new way ahead. For Deux Mains, reflection has never been about dwelling on what's been lost, but about recognizing what's been gained: strength, clarity, and conviction. It reminds us that even when everything feels uncertain, purpose gives us direction. For me, reflection became the foundation of renewal, the moment when faith replaced fear, and service replaced scarcity.

The Art of Renewal Through Purpose

Renewal isn't found in perfection, it's discovered in the willingness to begin again. In Haiti, renewal happens in small, deliberate acts, in the rhythm of a sewing machine and the quiet confidence of an artisan who knows their craft can change the course of a life. Renewal is more than a guiding principle, it's a lived experience. The brand may have been born as a response to economic hardship, but it has now grown into a sustainable enterprise built on empowerment.

That belief runs through every layer of Deux Mains. It's embedded in its mission to create lasting impact for the artisans who bring each collection to life. They earn fair wages, support their families, and invest in their futures, proving that when craftsmanship and compassion intersect, fashion can be both beautiful and just.

From Loss to Legacy

That message comes to life in my book, *From Loss to Legacy: How a Fashion Business Rose from Haiti's Rubble*. It tells the story of how compassion, community, and conscious business can transform devastation into dignity. The book reflects not only Deux Mains' evolution but a deeply personal belief, that rebuilding the world starts with rebuilding ourselves.

Every page is a reminder that renewal is not a destination; it's a daily decision.

Living the Lesson: Renewal as a Lifelong Practice

As we close another year, I've learned that the art of renewal is less about reinvention and more about remembrance, remembering who we are, why we started, and what matters most.

If you're standing in a season of uncertainty, start by reflecting on what has survived within you. Renewal often begins with a single act of courage: choosing to move forward, no matter how small the step.

Key takeaways for renewal:
- Reflect, don't react: growth begins with stillness.
- Anchor your purpose in service and gratitude.
- See renewal not as an outcome but as an ongoing practice.

Renewal is stitched into everything we make, a reminder that beauty can rise from brokenness, and purpose can be found in every new beginning. So, as you reflect on your own year, do it with grace. The challenges you faced weren't detours; they were directions leading you toward your own unstoppable power within.

Becoming An Unstoppable Woman Magazine

Connect With Julie
www.loss-to-legacy.com
www.instagram.com/deuxmains_official

December 2025

Becoming An Unstoppable Woman Magazine

THE RIPPLE EFFECT OF GRATITUDE:

HOW REFLECTION CAN CREATE MOMENTUM FOR WHAT'S NEXT

December 2025

By **Sabine Hutchison**

When I think about growth, I don't think about speed. I think about depth.

Our world still measures progress by how quickly we move, but I've learned that the most transformative changes happen when we slow down enough to notice what's already unfolding. Gratitude and reflection are the tools that make that possible.

Each December, I take time to pause before planning the new year. Instead of immediately setting goals, I start with questions: *What am I grateful for that I didn't expect this year? What moments taught me more than I realized at the time? Where did I surprise myself?*

This isn't just a ritual, it's a reset. Gratitude softens the pressure to be constantly improving and helps me see that growth doesn't always look like expansion; sometimes it looks like integration.

As a CEO, author, and founder, I've found that gratitude turns reflection into momentum. When I focus on what's working (the people, ideas, and experiences that bring meaning to my work), it strengthens my confidence to move forward with clarity.

Reflection without gratitude can become analysis.

Gratitude turns it into appreciation, and appreciation fuels action.

One of the most powerful lessons I've learned from The Ripple Network community is that gratitude connects us to each other. Every conversation, collaboration, or shared challenge ripples outward. When women celebrate not only their wins but also their lessons, we normalize the idea that reflection is progress. Gratitude creates permission to grow at your own pace, to honor your energy, and to find joy in small moments of alignment.

Over the years, I've adopted a few practices that keep this perspective alive, even during busy seasons:

1. **The Gratitude Mirror** – At the end of each week, I write down one thing I'm proud of that no one else noticed. This helps me stay connected to quiet progress, the kind that doesn't always show up on a to-do list.
2. **The Ripple Note** – I send a short message to someone who made a difference in my week. It could be a colleague, friend, or team member. Acknowledging others creates an ongoing ripple of gratitude that builds community and trust.
3. **The 10-Minute Reset** – Once a day, I pause without multitasking. No phone, no meetings. Just reflection. Those ten minutes often spark more clarity than an entire afternoon of planning.

These small moments of gratitude remind me that reflection is not about looking back; it's about grounding forward.

As the year closes, find your own version of stillness, not as a slowdown, but as a recalibration. Gratitude isn't the opposite of ambition; it's what gives ambition purpose. That's the ripple, not motion for motion's sake, but mindful movement that lasts.

When you combine gratitude with reflection, you don't just end the year stronger, you begin the next one aligned, present, and ready to lead from a place of wholeness.

That's how the ripple continues. Not through constant motion, but through mindful momentum.

Connect With Sabine

www.sabinehutchison.com
www.theripplenetwork.com
www.linkedin.com/in/sabinehutchison

Becoming An Unstoppable Woman Magazine

LETTING GO AND EMBRACING NEW BEGINNINGS

By **Bonnie Madani, Esq.**

December 2025

I started my career with the mindset that loyalty was the foundation of professional success. I whole-heartedly believed that I had to stay on course, work hard, and my dedication would ultimately speak for itself. I spent a couple of years at a law firm that I loved, one that once aligned deeply with my values and my approach to serving clients and the community. The people at the firm were great, the work we did was meaningful and fostered a strong sense of purpose and community.

With time, though, something shifted with that firm. There were subtle changes that created a snowball effect. Changes in leadership led to changes in culture and then to changes in priorities. This created a disconnect between who I was as a lawyer and what the firm was becoming. In short, the focus at this firm started to shift away from the empathy-driven advocacy that first inspired me to join the legal field and drew me to the firm. After that realization, every day I showed up to work, I was reminded that I had outgrown the space.

The realization was uncomfortable. I had invested my time, energy, loyalty, and identity to a firm that no longer fit my ideals. Maybe I stayed too long, afraid of change. Eventually, the truth became clear to me. If I stayed, I would be silencing my voice and, above all, my values.

By leaving, I walked away from stability, from a brand I helped strengthen, and from friendships that I valued deeply. To find that renewal I was looking for, I first had to find courage and clarity. I faced a lot of self-doubt, but I had to let go. After all, the act of letting go and releasing what no longer serves you is an act of faith not an act of failure. I had faith that there was something more waiting for me.

This leap of faith led to finding my new professional home at Downtown L.A. Law Group, a law firm that checked every single box of what I was looking for. Here, client care is a priority, collaboration is genuine, and every member of the team, from paralegals to senior partners, is valued for their contributions. Honestly, the alignment between purpose and practice feels seamless, and I can honestly say that I found a place where I can lead with integrity and empower others to do the same.

During this journey, I learned that renewal isn't about starting over, it's about realigning. It's about recognizing when your environment no longer supports your growth and having enough self-awareness and courage to let go in search of something different. The power of reflection lies in the revelation of what is out of balance and ultimately leads you back to your authentic self.

As I close this year and look ahead, I am filled with gratitude, for the lessons, the discomfort, and the courage to act and let go of *"a sure thing,"* no matter what it is. Growth is not always linear, instead it can be a cycle of evaluating, releasing, and renewing. We need to trust that our next step will be met with purpose, we just have to be brave enough to take it.

To anyone standing at a crossroads wondering whether it is time to move on, I say listen to yourself. You do not have to leave everything behind when you let go. You can carry forward everything you have learned and create space for what is meant to come next.

Connect With Bonnie

www.downtownlalaw.com/attorney-profiles/bonnie-madani
www.linkedin.com/in/bonnie-madani-3532a7102

FENIX TV

YOUR PLATFORM, YOUR VOICE, YOUR POWER!

STEP INTO THE SPOTLIGHT AS A HOST ON FENIX TV!

Are you ready to amplify your message, inspire others, and be part of a groundbreaking network dedicated to empowering women worldwide? FENIX TV is your platform to shine as a host, share your expertise, and connect with a global audience.

WHY HOST ON FENIX TV?

- Reach a worldwide audience passionate about empowerment
- Showcase your voice, brand, and expertise
- Join a community of inspiring leaders and changemakers
- Be part of a network that uplifts and celebrates women

Whether you dream of leading a talk show, sharing powerful stories, or educating and inspiring others—FENIX TV is where your voice matters!

SECURE YOUR SPOT TODAY!

Contact us now at
info@fenixtv.app

Learn more at
https://fenixtv.app

THE SHE RISES STUDIOS

PODCAST

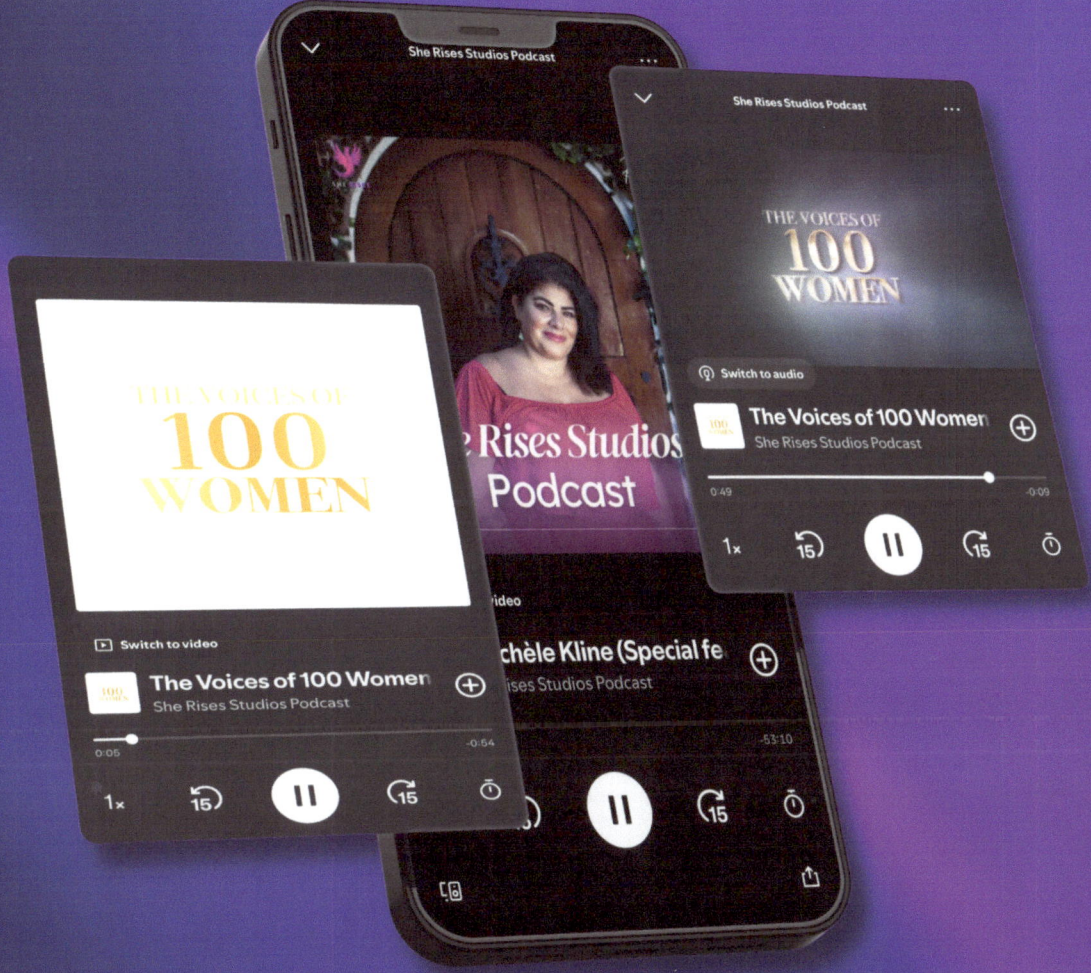

Each episode of the She Rises Studios Podcast delivers real stories, expert insights, and actionable strategies to help you step into your power and create the life you desire. This isn't just a podcast—it's your roadmap to confidence, success, and purpose.

Through powerful interviews with trailblazing entrepreneurs, thought leaders, and inspiring women, we dive deep into conversations that spark growth, fuel ambition, and ignite your potential. If you're ready to rise higher and live boldly, you're in the right place.

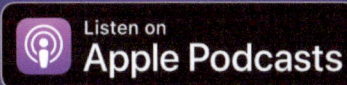 

SUBSCRIBE NOW AND START YOUR JOURNEY TO EMPOWERMENT!

Becoming An Unstoppable Woman Magazine

December 2025

THE POWER OF COMMUNITY AND SISTERHOOD:
BUILDING MEANINGFUL CONNECTIONS AND THE RIGHT SUPPORT NETWORKS

By **Melissa Gonzalez**

In many ways, my medical journey and the process of writing have been testaments to the power of community and sisterhood. Being 3,000 miles from home when I was jolted out of sleep and rushed to the ER, I was surrounded not by my biological family but by the unwavering care of my local work family and my chosen family that mobilized immediately to support me. They took shifts around the clock to ensure I had everything I needed to fill in the gaps until my husband and daughter could join me. My sister-in-law in California and my best friend from college (who was living in New York) booked flights without hesitation— choosing action over permission— to stand by my side when my husband had to travel back and forth with my daughter and while my parents couldn't travel due to being homebound with COVID.

These moments of support were not just acts of kindness; they were demonstrations of the immense power of connection and humanity that binds people together. Similarly, the women who cheered for and contributed to my book have shown me the beauty of collective strength. By sharing their vulnerabilities, experiences, and wisdom, they've elevated this project into a mini movement exemplary of the transformative potential of community. Their stories underscore a truth I've come to embrace: our connections with others can be our greatest sources of strength, insight, and resilience.

Through my life journey, I've come to appreciate how these varied connections enrich our lives. In professional spaces like DealMakeHers, I've experienced relationships that transition seamlessly from tactical business discussions to deeply personal conversations about mental wellness and self-care. Whether at a salon-style gathering at the New York apartment of Mindy Grossman, or at a book launch event at Stacy Bern's office, or standing at the NASDAQ ringing the opening bell together, or together for a 48-hour trip like those masterminded by Nancy Berger, where we experience everything from deep breathwork to cold plunges and multi-hour hikes, together we undergo deep individual exploration as an intimate group for both personal development as well as collective empowerment.

Outside of professional networks, personal friendships provide a different kind of nourishment. There are the people who mobilize at a moment's notice when "duty" calls — physically or digitally— offering exactly what you need, whether that's calm guidance, spiritual insight, or the simple joy of letting loose. Some will be your 911 call (Alice Kim, founder of PerfectDD, calls this your 911 Circle), filled with friends who can handle intense situations with calm and tactical means; some will be your deeply spiritual warriors who can go deep with you when you need it; some will be the friends you just need to let dance on tables and get a little crazy, channeling your forever youthful energy; some will see you for all that you are, every gift and every flaw and embrace all elements; some may only understand fractions of you but that's okay because those are your fractions of deepest connection with them and where you need them most. Some will have the gift of seeing life through rose-colored glasses, no matter what you tell them; others will be your tough love friends who provide the healthy tension you need in certain moments to challenge you and bring out the best in you, fostering your growth.

Together, all the pockets of people in our life form a mosaic of support that meets us where we are and challenges us to be our best.

From personal to professional, women-oriented communities like Luminary, founded by Cate Luzio, and DealMakeHers, founded by Stacy Berns, Stacey Widlitz, and Mary Ann Domuracki, further remind us that shared vulnerability can transform relationships into reservoirs of strength and inspiration. In these spaces, individual well-being is nurtured alongside collective growth, creating opportunities for like- minded connection and mutual uplift. They let us ask questions without judgment, open doors for one another, and gain confidence in asking for the things we want.

"We need to prioritize building relationships with other women. It's not a nice to have, it's not just a 'girl power kind of thing.'" — Kelly Hoey, author, Build Your Dream Network

This is how social science plays out: If you have big aspirations, whether you are an entrepreneur, a lawyer, rising in the ranks of management, an educator, or seeking to succeed in a creative industry, studies show that the women who achieve more of what they are seeking, in comparison to their equally talented and ambitious peers, are those who prioritize networking with other women. In pursuit of our individual interests, if we operate differently and we prioritize networking with other women, we will collectively lift up more women.

When we learn to embrace the diversity of our relationships, we open ourselves to a broader spectrum of possibilities. These connections encourage us to pursue diverse interests, foster ambitions, and explore new perspectives without judgment. By weaving in and out of supportive networks, we create a life enriched by shared purpose, personal growth, and limitless potential. And we begin to embrace pockets of people who fuel personal goals and growth without stigmas.

Ultimately, what I've come to realize is that community and sisterhood are not just support systems, they are catalysts for resilience, growth, and transformation. The people we surround ourselves with, in both personal and professional spheres, shape our experiences, expand our perspectives, and hold up the mirror to our best selves. They show up in moments of crisis, celebration, and quiet reflection, reminding us that we are never truly alone in our journeys.

Excerpted with permission from the publisher, Wiley, from The Purpose Pivot: How Dynamic Leaders Put Vulnerability and Intuition into Action by Melissa Gonzalez. Copyright © 2026 by John Wiley & Sons, Inc. All rights reserved. This book is available wherever books and eBooks are sold.

Connect With Melissa

www.melissagonzalez.com
www.instagram.com/melsstyles
www.linkedin.com/in/melissagonzalezlionesque

Becoming An Unstoppable Woman Magazine

5 SIMPLE DAILY RITUALS
THAT REMIND US — AND THOSE AROUND US — THAT WE MATTER
(AND THE JOURNEY THAT TAUGHT ME WHY)

By **John R. Miles**

Feeling like we matter isn't just a childhood need — it's a lifelong one.

When I was five years old, a carefree game of tag ended in a shattering accident that left me with a traumatic brain injury, years of wearing an eye patch, and a severe speech impediment. As a result, I often felt odd, defective, and—worst of all—invisible. Every school day, while my classmates stayed in their English lessons, I walked alone across a field to meet with a speech therapist.

Over time, something remarkable happened. That therapist didn't just teach me how to speak more clearly — she taught me that my voice mattered. She treated me as capable before I believed it myself, and her kindness became the scaffolding on which I rebuilt my confidence.

That early encounter with compassion planted the seed for my debut children's book, *YOU MATTER, LUMA* (on sale February 24, 2026) — a heartwarming story that extends my larger mission: to create a ripple effect of mattering across generations. I want to remind people of all ages that kindness isn't a small thing — it's a force.

Those early struggles — and the grace I received from one person who chose to see me — became the foundation for everything I've gone on to do. They shaped my life's mission: to help others discover that no matter their struggles or differences, they are never invisible. They matter.

In our busy, distracted world, it's easy to forget that belonging begins with small, intentional actions — simple moments that tell us, *and those around us,* that we're seen and valued. Here are five quick rituals that fit into any schedule — gentle reminders that who we are already makes a difference.

1. Begin with Gratitude, End with Reflection

Each morning, think of one person who makes your life brighter. Each night, text or tell them. Recognition doesn't just strengthen connection — it affirms our shared humanity.

2. Eye Contact Over Screens

When someone talks to you, put the phone down. Offer your full attention. In a world of constant distraction, eye contact has become one of the rarest — and most powerful — forms of affirmation.

3. The Ripple Check-In

Ask yourself: *Who did I make feel seen today?*
It's a simple question that transforms mattering from an idea into a practice — one small ripple at a time.

4. Say *"Thank You"* Like You Mean It

Go beyond the words. Add the *why*.
"Thank you for noticing that detail — it really helped."
Specific gratitude turns routine interactions into moments of genuine connection.

5. End the Day with a *"You Matter"* Moment

Before bed, jot down three moments when you mattered today — or whisper to your child, *"I love who you are."* End the day reminding yourself, and those you love, that worth is not earned; it's inherent.

Every act of kindness, every moment of presence, every sincere word of thanks becomes part of the quiet ripple of mattering. The truth is, we all have the power to make someone feel seen — including ourselves. And when we do, we remind the world of something simple and extraordinary: we all matter.

Connect With John

www.johnrmiles.com
www.youmatterluma.com
www.x.com/John_RMiles
www.facebook.com/johnrmiles.com
www.youtube.com/channel/UCTLdXATpxf8LP3riC0_mkKw
www.instagram.com/john_r_miles
www.tiktok.com/john_r_miles

FROM ONE ORDINARY MOMENT TO A GLOBAL MOVEMENT

By **Caroline Boudreaux**
Founder of Miracle Foundation

When I boarded a flight to India 25 years ago, I had no idea my life and the lives of thousands of children were about to change forever. I was a successful television executive living what I thought was the dream. But a Mother's Day visit to an orphanage in rural India transformed everything. I'll never forget the moment a little girl named Sheebani wrapped her tiny arms around me, looked up with eyes full of light and longing, as I laid her on her wooden bed with no mother to tuck her in. That moment shattered me but sparked a movement that continues to this day.

That experience ignited the spark that became the **Miracle Foundation.** 5.4 million children live in orphanages around the world and 80% of them have a living parent that, if supported, could care for them. Our bold mission is: *A Family for Every Child in Our Lifetime.* Over the past two decades, we've worked to ensure every child has the opportunity to grow up in a safe, stable family. What began with one child in India has grown into a global movement transforming child welfare systems across India, the developing world and the United States.

But, how do we know they're safe and cared for the way they deserve? We all know that transformation requires more than good intentions; it requires innovation and proof. That's why we built **ThriveWell**, an AI-powered platform that tracks and improves child well-being across five key areas safety, health, education, family relationships, and emotional well-being. It gives social workers, caregivers, and policymakers the data and tools they need to make smarter, faster, and more compassionate decisions for children and families

In other words, we're making love measurable.

We've supported more than **80,000 children** so far and we're just getting started. What makes this work truly powerful is **collaboration.** We partner with governments, NGOs, and lived-experience experts, people who grew up in the very systems we're transforming. Their voices guide everything we do.

Together, we're shifting the focus from systems care **to family care**. We're moving away from fixing the symptom to **preventing the problem** in the first place. Through prevention, family reunification, and foster support, we're proving that **family is the most effective form of child protection there is.**

As a leader, I've learned that impact isn't about having all the answers, it's about being willing to ask the hard questions and listen deeply. How can we do better for children? How can technology serve humanity instead of the other way around? And how can each of us use our unique gifts to build a more compassionate world?

My advice to any woman reading this who feels that tug on her heart to make a difference: **don't wait until you feel ready**. There's no perfect time to start. You don't need to know everything, you just need to care enough to take the first step. Courage isn't the absence of fear; it's the decision to move forward anyway.

Today, I look at the faces of children who are home, safe, and loved because of this work, and I'm reminded that one person's decision to act can change thousands of lives. That's the beauty of being unstoppable, it's not about never falling down; it's about standing up, again and again, for what matters most.

Because when we give children the foundation of family, we give them the world.

Connect With Caroline

www.miraclefoundation.org
Instagram: @themiraclefoundation

SHE RISES STUDIOS

*U*NLEASH YOUR STORY

BECOME A PUBLISHED AUTHOR!

Have you ever dreamed of sharing your wisdom, experience, or passion with the world? **Now is your time!**

Publishing a book isn't just about writing—it's about **establishing your authority, inspiring others, and creating a lasting legac**y. Plus, with the **$138.5 billion book industry** booming, there's never been a better moment to step into the spotlight.

At **SRS Publishing**, we don't just publish books—we **elevate voices, empower authors, and create change-makers**. Our mission is to help women break barriers, amplify their stories, and thrive in the publishing world. Whether you're an entrepreneur, thought leader, or storyteller at heart, **we're here to guide you every step of the way.**

JOIN THE FASTEST-GROWING PUBLISHING HOUSE FOR WOMEN IN THE USA.

READY TO TURN YOUR DREAM INTO REALITY?

 www.SheRisesStudios.com | contact@sherisesstudios.com

INSPIRE
EMPOWER
EDUCATE

CELEBRATING WOMEN'S RESILIENCE THROUGH GRATITUDE AND EMPOWERMENT

By **Jessica Hawthorne-Castro**

Women are naturally resilient. That strength is often rooted in how we're raised, the values that shape us, and the way we meet challenges head-on. Growing up in the Midwest, I was grounded in those values — hard work, integrity, and humility. Those early lessons became the foundation that allowed me to take bold risks later in life and to lead with both resilience and gratitude.

One of the most defining moments in my journey came when I made the decision to transition from being a Hollywood agent to joining a 20-year-old advertising agency that was in need of a new strategic direction. At the time, I was thriving in the talent representation world, championing creative voices and helping bring their stories to life. Then, unexpectedly, an employee from the agency — which was owned by a family member — approached me and asked what I thought the company's next chapter should be, and whether I would ever consider joining. It was a question that stopped me in my tracks and prompted deep reflection about my future and the kind of impact I wanted to make.

Switching careers and industries was not an easy decision to make. The advertising world was a shift from the entertainment world I knew so well, yet something inside me urged me to take that leap of faith. I leaned on the same core values that had guided me throughout my life — integrity, curiosity, and collaboration — trusting they would continue to serve me well in this new chapter. Over time, I realized that at their core, both careers shared a powerful common thread: in Hollywood, I had represented creative talent and helped build their individual brands; in advertising, I now represented companies and helped grow entire businesses. Though the audiences were different, the heart of the work — championing stories, shaping narratives, and driving growth — remained the same.

It turns out, once I joined Hawthorne Advertising, I quickly discovered a deep passion for creativity, strategy, and human connection. I fell in love with the fast-paced environment, the energy of the work, and the opportunity to deliver tangible, measurable results for clients. Every campaign became an opportunity to bring ideas to life, to connect people through storytelling, and to make an impact. I realized that when you truly love what you do, it doesn't feel like work — it feels like purpose in motion.

That decision to embrace a new career path led to an even bigger one.

In 2014, I made the choice to acquire Hawthorne Advertising outright — at full market value and without financing. It was a bold move that required both courage and conviction. Without outside investors or a safety net, I was fully accountable for the company's future. It was a test of not only business acumen but also inner strength. Looking back, that decision was pivotal. It taught me that true leadership isn't about playing it safe — it's about trusting your instincts, embracing risk, and staying aligned with your purpose.

Leadership, I've learned, is not defined by a title but by the willingness to make difficult choices, to guide others through uncertainty, and to continue learning with humility and grace. Every challenge — from changing industries to owning a company — strengthened my belief that resilience and gratitude are powerful partners in both leadership and life.

As we approach the 40th anniversary of Hawthorne Advertising, I'm incredibly proud of the impact we've had on the performance marketing industry. The brands we've helped grow, the companies we've guided to go public, and the countless consumers whose lives we've touched have all been deeply rewarding.

Yet above all, what stands out most are the relationships we've built — with our clients, partners, and employees. Creating a workplace grounded in support, respect, and genuine happiness has been one of the most gratifying achievements of all.

As I reflect on my journey, I see a clear throughline: resilience rooted in values, courage shaped by gratitude, and empowerment born from trusting yourself enough to take the leap. That, to me, is what it means to rise — and to become unstoppable.

Connect With Jessica

www.hawthorneadvertising.com
www.instagram.com/wearehawthorne
www.facebook.com/wearehawthorne
www.linkedin.com/company/wearehawthorne
www.instagram.com/jhawthornecastro
www.x.com/hawthornecastro
www.linkedin.com/in/jessicahawthornecastro

ART OF THE RENEWAL

By **Melva LaJoy Legrand**

My mother Joyce once said to me, *"Melva LaJoy, the past has passed, and knowing that is the first step."* In my experience, the art of renewal can feel like a personal mammoth for these reasons:

- We are comfortable with the known. It is where we believe we are valued, because to date, we hold on tightly to the wins of our current reality.
- We are uncomfortable with change because it may ask more of us, and we are unsure we are ready. In these moments, we forget that life is a book and we are meant to create new chapters because every day in life is preparing for the next plot twist.
- We allow our unresolved disappointments to prevent us from seeing any other possibility. When we work while carrying our disappointments, we mislabel them as "This is why I am strong," rather than the truth, which can be: "This is why I no longer dream," and the big one: "This is why I can't try again."
- We share with someone in our circle our potential new beginning and are met with skepticism. This usually sounds like: Are you sure? Have you considered all the options?" When you hear some version of this advice, especially from someone close to you, it is hard to reconcile that this advice has no meaning. What is probably true is that this person is also comfortable with you in the version they know. If you embrace something new, they would have to consider where they fit in and begin a renewal journey they are not ready for.

And when these things are true, starting a new chapter starts to feel impossible because we have not positioned ourselves to believe that we deserve more. Comfortability becomes a cage.

In order to embrace new beginnings, I think you need to do one thing: Dream. I mean this sincerely; let your mind run wild and explore these questions:

- Who do I want to be in this new chapter of my life? How do I want to feel? Who do I want to be around? And, equally important, what do I no longer want in my life? With this framework, you will be equipped to embrace your new endeavor with curiosity.

What is the worst that can happen? Often, we talk ourselves out of a good idea because we have decided—based on past experiences, poor advice, or just plain old fear—that our good idea isn't great enough.

But what if great was not the standard? What if you approached renewal without seeking another award on your tour of *"My Perfect Life,"* which does not exist, by the way. Rather, what if you embrace that the worst is not a final stop, but rather an opportunity for discovery, learning, and clarifying who you want to become. That mindset shift will allow you to embrace a new beginning without attaching it to your overall worth.

When you take these steps, I believe you will begin to look at your past as a wise advisor; your experiences have led you to discoveries. Your disappointments have sharpened your discernment, and your successes have reminded you why life's journey in itself is a form of art.

What I believe is that you are your most important resource, and also, you are your longest relationship, which is why, just like a performance review, you deserve to do a purpose or passion review; you deserve multiple moments of renewal because *living is the art, a*nd ultimately, you can be in full control of your masterpiece.

Connect With Melva

www.melvalajoylegrand.com
www.instagram.com/belajoyful

TWO VALUES, ONE CLEAR PATH:
HOW TO END THE YEAR WITH WHAT MATTERS MOST

By **Ginger Houghton, LMSW**

December always feels like both a mirror and a doorway. The lights go up, the world slows down (barely), and we start to take stock — of our work, our relationships, our hearts. We tally what we did, what we didn't, and the lessons that landed like lightning bolts.

For me, 2025 has been one of those years that brings you to your knees — hard in business, harder personally. In May, my family faced a health crisis with one of my kids, and when your child isn't okay, nothing else matters. I stepped away from work to focus where it mattered most, and for the first time, my leadership became about letting go.

Here's the humbling truth: when I stepped back, everything didn't fall apart — it actually got better. The systems, the trust, the shared leadership we'd been building for years finally had room to breathe. The team stepped up. Our nonprofit partner, Serenity Oaks Equine Sanctuary, flourished. Our impact grew.

It turns out, I wasn't the lynchpin. I was the bottleneck.

And realizing that? Whew. It'll shake you. Because once you see it, you can't unsee it — but fixing it isn't as simple as saying, *"I'll just do less."* You can't stop being the bottleneck if you keep leading the same way.

Real change means leading differently, not just working differently.

That realization cracked something open in me. I started asking what actually drives sustainable, soul-level growth — the kind that shows up in calm confidence and culture, not just numbers. And what I found was this: we can't move toward everything at once.

I used to live by a laundry list of values — service, creativity, courage, connection, family, learning, joy — all noble, all exhausting. Living by twelve values is like trying to lead twelve companies at once. Nobody wins.

Then, through Acceptance and Commitment Therapy (ACT), I learned something that stopped me in my tracks: we can really only move toward one or two values at a time. Two. That's it.

It sounds simple, but it's harder than you'd think. The moment you choose, you realize how much of your identity is tangled up in trying to be all the things. But the truth is, two values — the right two — change everything. They give you clarity, direction, and peace.

In June, in the quiet of my forced sabbatical, I asked myself: What matters most right now?

The answer came easily — presence and trust.

Presence meant being fully with my family — no divided attention, no half-listening while checking Slack. Trust meant believing my team could not only handle things but handle them beautifully. And they did.

Our business didn't just survive; it flourished. Staff found new autonomy. Serenity Oaks thrived. Our programs expanded, and our shared mission deepened. All because I stopped trying to do it all and started living from two clear, steady values.

That's the paradox of reflection and renewal: when you let go of what's extra, what's essential grows stronger.

So as you close this year, I invite you to do the same. Write down ten values that matter to you — the ones that tug at your heart — then circle two. The two that feel most alive for this season of your life.

Ask yourself: If I led, loved, and decided from just these two, what might change?

Because reflection alone doesn't create growth — alignment does. Gratitude gives us perspective, but clarity gives us freedom.

I'm walking into the new year with those same two values — presence and trust — tattooed invisibly on my heart. They're my compass for leading my company, my family, and myself.

We don't become unstoppable by doing more.

We become unstoppable by doing what matters — on purpose, with heart wide open.

Connect With Ginger

www.brightspottherapy.com
www.facebook.com/TherapyFarmingtonHills
www.instagram.com/brightspottherapymichigan
www.linkedin.com/company/89674352
www.tiktok.com/@brightspottherapy

she wins
WOMEN'S NETWORK

Elevate your business with the power of community.

Get access to the tools, connections, and support you need to grow—with a circle of women who truly get it.

WHAT'S INCLUDED

- Strategic networking & mentorship
- Expert-led masterclasses & exclusive resources
- Member spotlights, VIP perks & more

Join for just
$87/MONTH
no contracts, cancel anytime.

www.shewinswomensnetwork.com

JOIN THE SHE RISES STUDIOS COMMUNITY

SCAN TO JOIN

Daily motivation, expert insights, and sisterhood support come together in one empowering space. Connect, empower, and thrive—whether you're an entrepreneur, professional, or simply seeking inspiration, this is your place to grow!

You don't have to do it alone—let's rise together!

RESILIENCE THROUGH REINVENTION:

MY JOURNEY FROM CORPORATE LIFE TO COMMUNITY IMPACT

By **Jessica Fernandez**

One thing I've come to realize is that reinvention isn't always a choice, it's often a calling. For many women, the decision to pivot careers or lifestyles stems from a deeper desire to align their work with their values, passions, and purpose. My own journey is a testament to that transformation.

After years in corporate America, I found myself questioning the path I was on. I was burnt out—emotionally, mentally, and physically exhausted. The structure, pace, and pressure to meet monthly goals and quotas felt increasingly disconnected from the life I wanted to lead. I had built a successful career, but something was missing. I felt no joy or passion for the work I was doing. I craved impact. I wanted my work to matter, not just to the bottom line, but to real people and real communities.

So, I made the leap. I left the corporate world behind and stepped into the real estate field that, at first glance, seemed like a practical pivot. But for me, it was more than a career change. It was a platform. Real estate gave me the opportunity to help families find stability and a place to call home. It allowed me to build long-term relationships and grow a business rooted in service.

At the same time, I deepened my commitment to advocacy work in my community. I began volunteering with local organizations focused on economic mobility, domestic violence, poverty, mental health, housing access, and support for ALICE (Asset Limited, Income Constrained, Employed) households. I joined advisory committees, participated in research initiatives, supported fundraisers, and used my voice, and love for writing—to elevate the missions behind causes I care deeply about.

This dual path: real estate and advocacy, has honestly been both challenging and rewarding. I've had to learn new skills, build new networks, and redefine success on my own terms. There were moments of doubt, especially early on, when the safety net of a corporate paycheck was gone and the road ahead felt uncertain. But with each step, I discovered a deeper resilience. I wasn't just reinventing my career, I was reclaiming my purpose, taking my power back.

Reinvention isn't about abandoning your past; It's about building on it. My corporate experience gave me discipline, strategic thinking, and a strong work ethic. I've carried those tools into every client meeting, community forum, fundraiser, and initiative I've helped lead. The difference now is that I'm using those tools in service of something authentic, fulfilling, and meaningful. It lifted my spirit and elevated my confidence. I now wake up excited for the day ahead.

I've also learned that reinvention thrives in community. I've been inspired by other women who've made bold pivots—teachers turned entrepreneurs, nurses turned wellness coaches, mothers turned movement leaders. We share stories, offer support, and remind each other that it's never too late to start again.

Resilience through reinvention is not a straight line. It's a mosaic of courage, clarity, and connection. It's about listening to that inner voice that says, *"There's more for you out there,"* and having the guts to follow it. It's about turning uncertainty into possibility and using every setback as a stepping stone. Persistence is key.

Today, I'm proud of the life I've built. I'm proud of the homes I've helped families find, the policies and research I've helped shape, and the voices I've helped amplify. Reinvention isn't just a career move —it's a declaration and act of self-love. Because we are more than our job titles and roles. We are creators, changemakers, and leaders. And when we choose to pivot, we don't just change our lives, we inspire others to do the same.

Connect With Jessica

www.jessicafernandeznj.com
Instagram: @jessie4211
TikTok: @jessie42111
www.facebook.com/jessica4211

REFLECTION & RENEWAL:
RECLAIMING POWER THROUGH PURPOSE

By **Jessica Fernandez**

As the year winds down, I find myself reflecting not just on what I have accomplished, but on how I have grown. This season invites us to pause, take inventory of our inner lives, and ask deeper questions: What did I learn? What did I release? What do I want to carry forward?

For me, this year has been about reclaiming power through purpose and using my voice to advocate for causes I care deeply about. Nearly five years ago, I left corporate America after reaching my breaking point—burnt out, emotionally drained, and living with constant anxiety. I climbed the ladder, met the quotas, and checked every box. But inside, I felt hollow. I was not living, I was surviving.

That realization led to a bold pivot. I walked away from the security of a corporate paycheck and stepped into the world of real estate and community advocacy. It was not just a career change—it was a soul shift. I wanted my work to matter, not to corporate higher-ups, but to real people and communities.

The transition was not easy. It required deep reflection, uncomfortable honesty, and a willingness to start over. I faced unexpected challenges, including a partner struggling with addiction and increasingly abusive behavior. But through it all, I discovered something powerful: renewal does not come from external validation, it comes from within. It is born in the quiet moments when we choose ourselves, even when the path ahead is uncertain.

Mindfulness became my anchor. I began each morning with intention—journaling, meditating, or simply sitting in silence. These practices helped me tune out the noise and reconnect with my inner compass. I learned to listen to my body, honor my boundaries, and trust my intuition. It was not easy at first, but consistency led to transformation.

Gratitude was another game-changer. Instead of focusing on what I lacked, I celebrated what I had—my resilience, my relationships, my home, my children, my healing, and my growth. I kept a gratitude journal, jotting down three to ten things each day that made me feel grounded. Over time, this simple habit alone rewired my entire mindset. I stopped chasing perfection and started embracing progress, both big and small.

Purposeful and inspired action followed. I got involved with local organizations supporting ALICE (Asset Limited, Income Constrained, Employed) households, domestic violence survivors, and mental health initiatives. I used my voice to advocate for change, my skills to serve others, and my story to inspire hope. Every step I took was rooted in alignment, with who I am and what I stand for. I began to feel more alive and fulfilled in my life.

As women, we often carry the weight of expectations at work, at home, in society. But reflection and renewal remind us that we are more than these roles. We are creators, leaders, and healers. We have the power to rewrite our stories, reclaim our time, and redefine success on our own terms.

So, as the year comes to an end, I invite you to pause and listen to your inner voice. Reflect on your journey, both the wins and the lessons. Celebrate your growth, honor your truth, and envision the life you want to create. Whether you are pivoting careers, healing from loss, or simply seeking more joy, know this: your power lies within. You are worthy. You are powerful. You are resilient. You are loved. If you walk into the new year with this intention, trust me, you will become unstoppable.

Connect With Jessica

www.jessicafernandeznj.com
Instagram: @jessie4211
TikTok: @jessie42111
www.facebook.com/jessica4211

BRUNCH & BOSS UP™

Brunch & Boss Up™ is not your average talk show—it's a bold, live YouTube experience filmed at high-energy brunch events across the U.S. Designed for the modern entrepreneur, each episode brings together a rotating cast of inspiring business owners, thought leaders, and creatives for real, unfiltered conversations in front of a live audience.

Expect candid stories, fun games, and breakthrough moments—served with mimosas, good food, and great company.

A LIVE BRUNCH SHOW ABOUT REAL ENTREPRENEURS, REAL STORIES, AND BOSS-LEVEL ENERGY

WHERE ELSE CAN YOU SIP MIMOSAS, SHARE STORIES, AND SPARK BREAKTHROUGHS OVER BRUNCH?

Brunch & Boss Up™ is a bold new live YouTube show filmed at high-energy brunch events across the U.S.—where entrepreneurs, creatives, and change-makers come together to eat, laugh, connect, and rise.

Hosted by Hanna Olivas and Adriana Luna Carlos, founders of She Rises Studios and FENIX TV, the show is a natural extension of their mission to empower women globally through storytelling, media, and community. Together, they create spaces where women feel seen, heard, and inspired to lead boldly.

Each episode is filmed in front of a live audience and features a rotating lineup of powerhouse guests who bring their stories, insights, and unfiltered truths to the table. It's where personality meets purpose, and where mimosas meet the mic.

From hilarious games and real conversations to unexpected breakthroughs, Brunch & Boss Up™ is equal parts fun, fierce, and uplifting.

Think Red Table Talk meets UpDating—with a shot of a mimosa and a whole lot of hustle.

Hosted by dynamic duo Hanna Olivas and Adriana Luna Carlos, the show brings their signature energy and heart to every city it touches. Each event is designed to celebrate connection, elevate voices, and create space for meaningful growth and collaboration.

Want to be part of the cast?

We're looking for 4–6 bold, dynamic entrepreneurs in each city to join the show.

As a featured cast member, you'll be:

- On stage, live with our hosts
- Part of the games, challenges, and conversations
- Featured on YouTube and across our social media
- Celebrated for your energy, personality, and story—not just your business

Brunch & Boss Up™ is coming to cities near you.

APPLY TO BE IN THE CAST

Info@SheRisesStudios.com

WE DIDN'T CHOOSE THIS STORY

By **Sharon T. Markey**

Nearly four years ago, our family lost everything except each other. What we've experienced and learned since has reshaped not only our lives, but the lives of many other women.

In December 2021, we were living in Kyiv, Ukraine. My husband and I had called Ukraine home for a combined five decades, and our six children had never lived anywhere else. When Russia invaded in February 2022, we made the wrenching decision to flee, leaving behind not just possessions but friends, relatives, and a faith community that was the backbone of our life there.

We crossed into Hungary, assuming we'd soon go back. Three chaotic weeks later, we settled into a cramped two-bedroom apartment in downtown Budapest. Reeling with loss, I focused on doing the next necessary thing—feeding my children, creating a cocoon of safety in a strange city, counting the days until we could return. I couldn't imagine then that we would not only build a new home, but help others build theirs too.

Compelled by love for Ukraine, even before we found permanent housing, we began asking, "How can we help?" We joined forces with a handful of other refugees and began visiting displaced families across Hungary. Driving from city to city, we quickly realized the greatest need wasn't food—it was connection.

We met mothers and children who were isolated and hopeless. From the very first trip it was obvious that these families, who truly had nothing, were more grateful for a visit from someone who spoke their language than for the groceries we brought. Many didn't know a single other Ukrainian in town. We began dreaming of drawing them together, so aid days turned into simple lunches. We met wherever we could find space: in churches, parks, cafes, and parking lots.

By the first Christmas, kind friends had given enough to buy gifts for the children. A wrapped present in a new country can't restore what war has stolen, but it can remind a child that he is seen. One mother sent us a photo of her little boy sleeping with the toy we'd given him.

Now, as we approach our fourth Christmas in exile, I feel a complicated gratitude. I still miss Ukraine fiercely—the language, the neighbors who became family, the courage that has inspired me to be more courageous myself—but we have a life in Hungary.

© VIKTORIA MOKRA

Many women and children we first served have moved on, but of those who stayed, many have become dear friends.

We've traded mass deliveries for presence. Our team now focuses on weekly visits with women in five cities. We drink tea around kitchen tables, swapping stories about our children's illnesses, job challenges, and the welfare of relatives still in Ukraine. We celebrate wins and sit with the hard things, even holding memorial services for loved ones whose lives were cut short by the war. We pray for each other and turn to the Bible, because that's where my hope has always been. Together we're learning to recognize the goodness of God amidst a world gone horribly wrong.

We didn't choose this story, but we do get to choose how to live inside it. =

For our family, that means staying present, listening more than we speak, and helping other women gather enough safety to start dreaming again. If the war ended tomorrow, we'd still carry these people and this place in our bones. Until then, we'll keep showing up—one day, one city, one shared meal at a time.

Connect With Sharon

www.SharonTMarkey.com
www.facebook.com/sharontmarkey
www.instagram.com/mommy.joys

RESILIENCE THROUGH REINVENTION:
HOW LOSS LED ME TO LIFE AS A DEATH DOULA

By **Sheila M. Burke**

When my husband passed away from cancer at just fifty-six, my world shattered. There's no graceful way to describe what it feels like to lose the person you built your life around. The quiet that follows—the hollow, echoing kind—is the kind of silence that forces you to confront who you really are, and what remains when everything else falls away.

In those early months, I was consumed by the kind of grief that strips you bare. I didn't recognize myself. My days were heavy, slow, and uncertain. Yet even in that darkness, something inside me said that this couldn't be the end of my story. I began to walk. First, down the street, then through the woods, and eventually, through life again. I didn't know it then, but those walks would become my medicine—movement for my body and balm for my spirit. I even hiked the camino de santiago and downed the grand canyon.

Grief is a strange teacher. It dismantles, but it also refines. Through my pain, I found myself drawn back to the bedside—this time, not as a wife, but as a companion to others in their final chapters. I became a death doula—someone who helps guide the dying and their loved ones through the end-of-life process with compassion, dignity, and peace.

My husband's death was my greatest heartbreak, but it was also the beginning of my calling. Sitting beside him, I witnessed the profound beauty that can exist even in dying—the small moments of laughter, forgiveness, and love that linger until the very last breath. I realized that death isn't something to fear or avoid. It's a sacred transition, one that deserves presence, tenderness, and truth.

Becoming a death doula wasn't a career change—it was a soul shift. It required me to reflect deeply on what I valued, what I could release, and what I was meant to carry forward. I had to let go of the need to control outcomes, the guilt of surviving, and the illusion that healing meant *"moving on."* True renewal came when I understood that grief isn't something you overcome—it's something you learn to walk alongside.

Through this work, I've learned that reflection is the birthplace of reinvention. When we take time to sit with our stories—the pain, the joy, the messiness—we uncover the strength that's always been within us. Reflection invites renewal. It teaches us to let go of what no longer serves us: the fear, the self-doubt, the old identities that no longer fit.

If I could offer one piece of guidance to anyone standing at the edge of their own transformation, it would be this: Don't rush your rebirth. Renewal isn't loud or dramatic. It's often gentle and slow, like when spring thaws a frozen creek. Allow yourself to pause. Listen. Reflect. What do you need to release to step into your next season?

For me, that meant allowing death to become my teacher—and my purpose. Today, I sit beside others as they take their final bow, helping families find grace in the hardest of moments. I write and teach about end-of-life care, grief, and legacy because I believe that understanding death helps us live more fully.

So as we step into a new year, I invite you to reflect on what your own season of loss or change has taught you. There is power in your reflection, there is peace in your letting go, and there is life—beautiful, unstoppable life—waiting on the other side of what you thought would break you.

Connect With Sheila

www.Endoflifedoulacle.com
Socials: @deathdoulaCLE

SHE RISES STUDIOS

Live Tour

10 CITIES. 2 WEEKS. EMPOWERING WOMEN EVERYWHERE.

JANUARY **12-26**   REGISTER NOW

100 WOMEN OF IMPACT™

THE DOCUSERIES THAT AMPLIFIES WOMEN'S VOICES

We just wrapped our first taping of 100 Women of Impact™ in San Diego, and the momentum has only just begun. This powerful docuseries is shining a spotlight on extraordinary women who are shaping the future through leadership, resilience, and influence.

Be part of the movement by sharing your story in an exclusive filmed interview for the docuseries. Gain visibility through red carpet experiences, media coverage, and distribution across She Rises Studios platforms, while connecting with a global network of women making an unstoppable impact.

NEXT FILMING OPPORTUNITIES

SHE WINS GLOBAL SUMMIT | LAS VEGAS | NOVEMBER 6–7, 2025
EMPOWERHER CONTENT DAY | LAS VEGAS | FEBRUARY 2026

SIGN UP TODAY

VISIT WWW.SHERISESSTUDIOS.COM/INTRODUCING-100-WOMEN-OF-IMPACT TO CLAIM YOUR SPOT.

FROM BREAKDOWN TO BREAKTHROUGH
- YEAR END REFLECTIONS

By **Katia Davis**
Intuitive Purpose Coach at Inner Rainbow Healing

This March, I found myself in the hospital after a panic attack- with a diagnosis of stress-induced anxiety and stress-induced depression. I knew I had a stressful job that was wearing on me, but I didn't realize how bad it really was until that moment.

Back in 2008, I became a teacher so I could travel the world. It was fun for about a decade. Then we settled in Hawai'i and I spent the next 7 years telling myself it would be my last year as a teacher.

I was building my own businesses on the side, trying to find the right thing for me that lit me up, made a difference in others' lives, and supported me.

I felt like having a steady teaching job with a steady paycheck was safe, but how safe can it be when it's putting me in the hospital?

They gave me a week off work and I stared at the ferns in our yard, journaled, and doodled little cartoons depicting my life. At the end of the week I made the decision not to go back and spent the next week grieving and commemorating all those years as a teacher and all those children.

I opened up more space on the calendar in my Reiki studio and found more people came in when I was open during the day (not exactly shocking).

But the more I practiced, the more I found Reiki in itself wasn't the right fit either. I could remove people's energy blocks, but what was truly needed was coaching to help them transform their energy so it didn't manifest in the same patterns and sticky spots. That is the work I do now- help people release their old blocks, figure out what really matters to them, and start living with more purpose and vibrancy.

It's been a tumultuous year with two rebirths, but I feel more alive and more aligned than ever before.

I wanted to share some journal prompts to help others who may be getting ready for a big transition too…

Reflection Journal Prompts:
- What was your biggest challenge in 2025?
- What would you like to leave behind in 2025?
- What/who would you like to forgive from 2025?
- What was the biggest lesson you learned in 2025?
- What was the greatest gift you received in 2025?
- What are you most proud of from 2025?

Looking Ahead Journal Prompts:
- What does your dream life look like? (eg. Where do you live? Who is part of your life? What do you do for work? What is in your bank account? What do you eat? How do you exercise/move? How do you fill your cup? How do you practice spirituality and/or creativity? How do you practice self-care? What are your hobbies? How do you feel?)
- How can you narrow the gap between your current life and your dream life in 2026? What actions can you (will you!) take?
- How will you take care of yourself this year? How will you show up for yourself? Accept yourself? Love yourself?
- How will you practice gratitude this year?
- What aspects of your highest self would you like to embody in 2026? What actions would you take as your highest self? Take them!
- What are your goals for 2026? How will you know when you've reached them? What steps will you take to reach them? *(goals are outcome-driven and measurable, and intentions are feeling- and theme-based)
- What are your intentions for 2026?
- Choose a one-word mantra as your guiding light for 2026 (you can always change it later!).

Connect With Katia
www.innerrainbowhealing.com
www.instagram.com/katia.innerrainbow
www.youtube.com/@innerrainbowhealing

THE ART OF RENEWAL

— LEARNING TO LOVE MYSELF, ONE SMALL PROMISE AT A TIME

By **Misty Gebhart**

For most of my life I tried to be invisible. I stayed small, kept the peace, and avoided mirrors like they were traps. I didn't take care of myself. I ate to numb, punished myself for every mistake, and sabotaged anything that looked like happiness. My daily routine was survival: coffee, maybe a shower, clothes passable enough for my teaching job, and a steady stream of self-criticism. I was a good teacher but a terrible friend to myself. Chaos was my normal, and I honestly believed I had no worth.

By 2019 I was exhausted. My life felt like a loop of bad decisions and emotional pain. One night, standing in that hopeless blur, I realized the only person who could change anything was me. I didn't know how to love myself, but I was willing to try. That single decision was the beginning of everything new.

My first promise was small: *brush your teeth every day.* It sounds ridiculous, but for me it was revolutionary. I had never thought I was even worth clean teeth. Every morning I forced myself up and kept that promise. One tiny act of care built the foundation for another. I started walking ten minutes a day on a treadmill, then outside. I ate food that nourished me. I slept—deep, healing sleep my body had been denied for decades of living in survival mode.

Letting go was harder. I had to unlearn the belief that my worth depended on keeping everyone else happy. I had been trained to believe that if I upset anyone, I was unlovable. Releasing that idea felt like peeling off my own skin. But slowly, I learned to take up space, to speak honestly, and to stop apologizing for existing.

A year into my self-love experiment, I hardly recognized the woman I'd become. I trained for and finished a half-marathon. I discovered that I love shoes, perfume, and dressing like I matter. I began standing up for myself in relationships, and eventually, I chose to leave the one that no longer fit the person I was becoming. For the first time in my life, I lived alone—free, safe, and proud of who I was.

Renewal, to me, isn't just about change. It's rebirth. It's deciding, over and over, to love yourself enough to start again. My transformation didn't happen overnight, but it began the moment I said, *I will love myself, no matter what that looks like.*

If my story sounds like yours—if you're caught in the same exhausting loop, avoiding your reflection, or speaking cruelly to yourself—I want you to know this: you are beautiful, you are amazing, and you are worthy. The way out begins with one tiny promise you keep to yourself. Brush your teeth. Take a walk. Drink a glass of water. Do something small and keep doing it.

That's how self-love grows—one kept promise at a time.

If my story were a Patchling, she'd be a purple eggplant named **Eggerly Glitterjoy**, born January 1st. Her affirmation would read: *"It's okay to take up space, speak your mind, and live in peace. Old habits may whisper, but truth always wins."*

Connect With Misty

www.InspiredChapter.com
Instagram: @ladymistyg
www.facebook.com/people/Lady-Mistys-Creations-LLC/100092741401604
TikTok: @ladymisty

© LAUREN HERRING, HERRING PHOTOGRAPHY HERRINGPHOTOGRAPHYSITE.COM

UNIVERSITY OF LEEDS

ENROLL FREE TODAY TO SCALE YOUR BUSINESS

She Rises Studios and Goldman Sachs 10,000 Women join forces to provide education, resources, and a supportive global community for women-led SMEs, empowering them to grow, innovate, and thrive in today's competitive landscape.

HOW I BROKE FREE FROM BEING A TOTAL INTROVERT AND PUT MORE FUN IN MY LIFE

By **Dr. Noelle Nelson**

I went to the movies a while back with a friend. It was billed as an action-comedy film, and I was looking forward to some good laughs. I loved the comedy parts, but the constant crashes and explosions overwhelmed me.

In typical extrovert fashion, my friend was revved up by the action, recharged by every bang and boom. I, in typical introvert fashion, wanted nothing more than to crawl into bed and recuperate from the nonstop sensory overload.

That's the difference between an introvert and an extrovert. An introvert thrives on inner stimulation--thinking, quiet reading and silence. An extrovert thrives on outer stimulation--parties, people and socializing. Total opposites. For many years, I used to hang out only with people whose personalities were similar to mine, doing the things that quiet folk enjoy. It made me comfortable. I never had to take chances and I always knew what to expect.

But it got boring. Sure, there's a lot less anxiety when you know how any given situation is going to play out. There's also a lot less fun, less newness, less adventure. Not that I ever wanted a lot of adventure, but a little would take the yawn out of my same-old, same-old life.

The result? Here am I, a die-hard introvert, realizing that if I wanted a full life, I had to stop playing it safe. I had to get out of my comfort zone and cultivate friendships with people opposite of me. I forced myself to develop interests in activities other than the nicely predictable.

I decided to enter competitive ballroom dancing. Learning ballroom dancing is a nice, quiet, introvert-perfect affair. But competition? That's another story.

My initiation into competitive ballroom dancing would rattle any introvert. Imagine a ballroom jammed with cheering, screaming people, simultaneously yelling out encouragement to their favorite contestant at full volume to be heard over the loud, never-ending music. The first few competitions were so introvert-challenging that I couldn't remember my steps and barely made it around the floor, hanging on for dear life to my partner--who afterward suggested gently, nursing a very sore hand, that a little less grip on my part would be advisable.

You'd think I'd run for the hills at that point: too many people, too much noise, too much stimulation. But amid it all, I had fun. It was the kind of fun I'd never experienced sitting on a beach reading a good book in quiet solitude. Instead, it was the kind of fun I'd had with my extroverted friend in the movie theatre laughing until my sides hurt.

Fun is what keeps me in the ballroom game. Fun is what makes me suck it up, learn how to engage with people radically different from myself, indulge in casual conversations about anything and everything (aka introvert-hell) and find the joy of dance amid the dizzying extroverted, somehow orderly, chaos of competition.

Try stepping out of your comfort zone—a little bit at a time. You will still be an introvert. Nothing will change that. What you will come to realize is that interacting and fostering friendships with people with all types of personalities can be wonderful. I now understand that the world is full of rich and diverse experiences we can each benefit from in one way or another. The more we appreciate and enjoy our differences, the more we enrich our own lives as well as the lives of others.

And yes, have a lot more fun along the way.

Connect With Dr. Noelle

www.noellenelson.com
www.facebook.com/Dr.NoelleNelson
www.threads.com/@meettheamazings

© TRINITY WHEELER PHOTOGRAPHY

BURNOUT TO BUBBLES

By **Carrie Speed**

I had reached the point where helping people started to feel like helping everyone but myself. I worked in social services in the child welfare field, loved the mission, but the emotional weight was a lot. I was exhausted, stretched thin, and wondering how I could keep doing meaningful work without completely losing my spark (or my sanity).

What I realized was that I didn't actually want to stop helping children. I just wanted to do it in a way that felt light, fun, and a little more like me. So instead of paperwork and crisis calls, I traded it for bubbles, music, and yoga mats.

That's how PlayMotion Kids came to life, a children's enrichment program that combines music, movement, and mindfulness for toddlers and preschoolers. Basically, we help little ones move, play, and breathe, and hopefully remind the grown-ups in the room to do the same.

Starting a business was not exactly a walk in the park. There were moments I thought, *"Wow, this might be the worst idea I've ever had,"* right before something amazing would happen, like a child saying, *"That was so much fun,"* after class. That's when I knew I was onto something.

What I love most about PlayMotion is that it's play at work. We end every class with a simple gratitude ritual: hands over hearts saying, *"Thank you, body, breath, and mind."* It's sweet, a little chaotic, and somehow deeply grounding. Kids start repeating it during lunch or nap time, and teachers tell me it changes the whole energy of their classroom. That's the kind of ripple effect I want to be part of.

Reinvention, I've learned, isn't about throwing away who you were before. It's about finding a new way to use what you already have, your skills, your heart, your experience, in a way that fits the life you actually want. Mine just happens to include a lot more singing, stretching, and pretending to be animals.

If you're feeling stuck or burned out, sometimes the answer isn't to work harder or push through. Sometimes it's to get quiet, reflect, and ask, *"What would feel lighter?"*

For me, that question led to creating a business that makes me smile every single day, one that helps kids build confidence, calm, and kindness through play.

It's still hard work (and yes, there are plenty of random egg shakers and colorful scarves in my car), but it's the good kind of tired, the kind that comes from doing something that fills you up instead of drains you.

So if you're in your own season of reflection, maybe this is your reminder that it's okay to start over, go sideways, or in a completely different direction. You don't need permission to reinvent yourself. You just need a little courage, a lot of curiosity, and maybe a reminder to have fun when it's gets hard.

Because sometimes resilience isn't about powering through. It's about remembering what lights you up and letting that be enough to guide the next step.

Connect With Carrie

www.playmotionkids.com

THE ART OF RENEWAL:
LETTING GO TO GROW FORWARD

By **Malaysia Harrell, LICSW, LCSW-C, BCD**

In every woman's life, there comes a sacred threshold, the moment between who she has been and who she is becoming. For Malaysia Harrell, that threshold was both painful and powerful. A decorated Air Force veteran, psychotherapist, spiritual transformation coach, keynote speaker and author, Malaysia has spent decades guiding others through healing and alignment. Yet, her most profound transformation began when she learned to do something counterintuitive for high-achieving women: to let go.

"The art of renewal," she says, *"isn't about striving for more, it's about surrendering what no longer serves you."*

Malaysia's journey from survival to soul alignment was not a straight path. It began during a season of physical and emotional unraveling, a time when her strength as a leader, a clinician, and a woman was tested to its core.

Through illness, transition, and the quiet ache of burnout, she found herself asking deeper questions about identity, purpose, and faith. The answer, she discovered, wasn't found in doing, but in being.

"I had to unlearn the idea that my worth was tied to my success," she reflects. *"Letting go of that belief was the beginning of my freedom."*

As the founder of Blissful Life Consulting and the Malaysia Harrell Foundation, Malaysia now teaches others how to experience this same liberation. Her work helps women leaders, especially veterans, caregivers, and high-performing professionals, reconnect to their truth through holistic wellness, mindfulness, and spiritual integration.

Through her research and lived experience, Malaysia developed a reflective framework she calls The Renewal Cycle, a four-step process for releasing, reflecting, realigning, and rising.

1. Release: The first step, she explains, is courageously identifying what you're still carrying that isn't aligned with who you're becoming, whether it's an old narrative, a fear, or a false sense of control. *"You can't rise with what's weighing you down,"* Malaysia says. *"Letting go is not losing; it's making room for what's next."*

2. Reflect: True reflection requires stillness. Malaysia integrates mindfulness practices and journaling prompts to help women listen deeply to their inner wisdom. *"Stillness reveals what striving hides,"* she shares. *"When we slow down, we see with new clarity where we've been operating from fear instead of faith."*

3. Realign: Renewal is not just about release; it's about redirection. Malaysia emphasizes aligning your intentions with your authentic values. Through forgiveness work, spiritual grounding, and visioning, women begin to design lives that feel good on the inside, not just impressive on the outside.

4. Rise: The final step is rebirth, walking boldly in your renewed identity. Malaysia's story itself is a testimony to this truth. After years of self-sacrifice and overextension, she redefined success on her own terms, one rooted in peace, purpose, and impact. Today, her leadership embodies both power and presence, reminding others that wholeness is the new wealth.

Her upcoming keynote talks, workshops, retreats, and foundation programs, are built around this philosophy, creating spaces for women to release, restore, and remember who they are beneath the masks of performance.

"As women, we often hold the world together," she says. *"But renewal invites us to hold ourselves with the same compassion, reverence, and care."*

Malaysia's message for the end of the year is clear: before you plan what's next, pause to honor how far you've come. Reflection and gratitude are not passive acts, they are portals for transformation.

"Every ending carries the seed of a new beginning," she writes in "God Has My Six", her upcoming memoir that chronicles her journey from trauma to transformation

"When we surrender the story of who we were, we make space for the woman we were always meant to be."

Through her voice and vision, Malaysia Harrell is redefining what it means to be unstoppable, not through endless striving, but through soulful renewal. Her story reminds us all that growth begins with release and that sometimes, the bravest act is simply letting go.

Connect With Malaysia

www.instagram.com/malaysiahharrell
www.facebook.com/share/15YFYAy18u/?mibextid=LQQJ4d
www.linkedin.com/in/malaysia-h-harrell-a322b19b
www.tiktok.com/@malaysiahharrell
www.youtube.com/@dreamlifemanifested
www.malaysiaharrell.com

PURE HEAVENLY HAIR BOUTIQUE

Matte Liquid Lip Gloss

Rich, long-lasting color meets a velvety matte finish. *Matte Liquid Lip Gloss* is perfectly pigmented and effortlessly chic, making every look a statement.

SHOP NOW | PUREHEAVENLYHAIR.COM

MORE WORKOUT, LESS TIME!

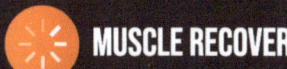 MUSCLE RECOVERY PAIN RELIEF STRESS REDUCTION WEIGHT LOSS

 INCREASED CALORIE BURN DETOXIFICATION LOWER BLOOD PRESSURE

 CELLULITE REDUCTION ANTI-AGING & SKIN REJUVENATION IMPROVED CIRCULATION

Becoming An Unstoppable Woman Magazine

A BOLD CREATIVE DECISION THAT CHANGED EVERYTHING

December 2025

By **Sufaiyah Taranum K**
Creative Director, Itzfizz Digital

When I decided to join **Itzfizz Digital**, I was stepping into a space that already had a strong foundation in growth and strategy. The agency was known for its digital expertise, yet I saw an opportunity to bring something deeper. My goal was to turn our creative work into a unified voice that expressed purpose and clarity across every brand we touched. It was a bold decision because transforming an existing culture requires both patience and conviction.

In my first few months, I focused on observing how creativity flowed through the team. We had incredible talent but scattered direction. My first strategic move was to create a **central design system** and a **consistent storytelling framework**. It was not about adding more rules but about creating rhythm and intent. When structure supports creativity, ideas grow faster and last longer.

The risks were real. Redefining creative processes in an already successful agency meant questioning habits that had worked in the past. It required honest conversations and trust-building. There were moments of resistance, especially when deadlines met experimentation. But progress often begins in discomfort. Over time, the results spoke louder than any presentation.

We began to see the shift in our work. Our visual identity became sharper, our campaigns carried stronger emotional threads, and our communication felt cohesive. The energy within the team changed, too. **Collaboration replaced competition.** Designers and writers began thinking beyond deliverables, focusing on impact. That transformation was the true reward of leadership.

Together, we have worked on **over one hundred brands**, each with a distinct story to tell. Brands like **Tipplr, Acenteus CCA, Loyora, Waterstone, Doctor Fizz, Shiva Manvi, Avia, and Axxonet** became creative journeys that taught us to see design as both expression and strategy. In total, the agency has now completed more than **two hundred fifty projects**, and each one reflects a piece of that collective evolution.

For me, creative leadership is not about control. It is about shaping systems that allow people to do their best work. My focus has always been to create an environment where creativity feels **safe, structured, and ambitious**. When a designer knows their voice matters, innovation becomes natural.

This journey has reminded me that bold decisions are rarely about instant results. They are about choosing direction over comfort. Joining Itzfizz was that choice for me. It challenged me to think, lead, and create differently. It taught me that **gratitude and resilience** are the real engines behind growth. Every creative decision we make is a step toward crafting a more intentional and meaningful story.

Connect With Sufaiyah

www.itzfizz.com
www.instagram.com/itzfizz_digital
www.linkedin.com/in/sufaiyah-taranum

REFLECTION & RENEWAL:
THE POWER WITHIN

By **Jennifer M. Ellis**

2025. A year I never expected. A year I never planned for. The end of 2024 found my husband struggling from an undiagnosed condition.

On February 4, 2025 his life ended.

What do I do now?
Grieve.

Live – I have two mortgages and a dog I am now solely responsible for.

I am a yoga, fitness, and meditation teacher. What would I tell one of my students?

I'd probably give them a hug and let them know I am here for them.

Maybe I should do that for myself.

Writing this, it has been almost 10 months. Yet, it feels like yesterday. Time has become …weird since Jim's passing.

I have had to find the power within.

Many days I have wanted to lay on the floor and stay there. Many days, I have been exhausted physically and mentally. Many days, I wanted to escape and pretend nothing had changed.

When you are a couple, you live in a way where you have joint goals, plans, schedules, shared tasks… and my husband and I were around each other pretty much 24/7 since we both worked primarily from home.

How do you get through the days?
Sometimes I don't know.

What I do know, is I keep to my personal practice every morning of yoga, Pilates, meditation, and prayer… followed by a couple Starbucks Pike Place roast coffees.

I have actually had some revelations in that morning practice such as the correlation between my previous dog's passing and that of my husband's, next steps in my life, what to do about certain home issues, and more.

The quiet, the presence, the tuning inward. The tuning inward. When your couple suddenly becomes one, you do not really remember what you alone want, need, think, and be.

Even now I'll go toward something that was what Jim and I enjoyed – and have to ask myself, do I enjoy doing this on my own now? And if the answer is no, having the choice to decide what would work best for me, since it is – only me now.

I have had to learn to balance my emotions with gratitude. Gratitude can truly turn a mood around. For example, thinking – I wish Jim was here to watch this Miami Dolphins game with me. I have found yes, acknowledge that I miss that, but instead of staying in that space of loss and upset where it affects the rest of my day – moving to something I am grateful for – like supporting Jim to live one of his dreams to go see a Miami Dolphins game from the sidelines on the field.

There is so much I can write on this, and I know there will be more in the future.

But in closing, renewal. The place I am in now. I must become me again. Not that I wasn't me with my husband – but standing alone is totally different. It is a reinvention of sorts, especially that this age (52). I will use the tools I teach, feel what needs to be felt, stay present with what is having faith in the future. Tapping into that power within through my practices of yoga, movement, and meditation. That power we all have but sometimes forget we have or do not remember how to access.

I celebrate all who have gone through transforming challenges of their own – it is hard work! You inspire me!

Connect With Jennifer

www.life-enlightenment.com
www.facebook.com/JenniferLifeEnlightenment
www.linkedin.com/in/jennifer-ellis-b01ba025
Twitter: @LifeEnlighten
Instagram: @JenniferMarieEllis

FROM SCARCITY TO STRENGTH:
HOW GRATITUDE RESHAPES YOUR RELATIONSHIP WITH MONEY

By **Maria Kamilla Gonzalez**
Co-founder, Finanzo.ca

As the year comes to a close, many of us feel the weight of unmet financial goals, rising costs, or the emotional burden of trying to provide for our families. For immigrants and first-generation wealth builders, that weight can feel even heavier.

But at Finanzo, we've learned that transformation doesn't always start with more money—it starts with a shift in mindset. And one of the most powerful mindset shifts is gratitude.

Gratitude isn't just a feel-good emotion; it's a proven tool for mental clarity and financial resilience. Studies show that people who practice gratitude experience lower levels of stress and anxiety, are more likely to stick with financial goals, and make more thoughtful spending decisions.

At Finanzo, we see this daily in our community: individuals who come to us feeling overwhelmed by debt or disconnected from their finances often begin to shift the moment they start acknowledging what *is* working in their lives.

From survival mode to strategic action

Financial scarcity can push us into survival mode, where every decision feels urgent and fear-based. Gratitude acts as a circuit breaker. It brings us back into the present and helps us recognize that while we may not be where we want to be, we are not powerless. *We have made progress. We have strengths. We have options.*

When people in the Finanzo program begin to regularly journal what they're grateful for—even if it's just being able to cover rent that month or learning one new concept about investing—they start to reclaim agency. That small shift opens the door to bigger changes: negotiating salaries, paying off debt, starting investment accounts, and helping others in their community do the same.

Client stories: from modest investments to multiple income streams

When Natalia moved to Canada, she learned to budget and understand the financial system. She understood that financial instruments such as Tax Free Savings Accounts and investment accounts were essential to growing wealth.

"Knowing how to manage money, not just earn it, changed everything. Going from zero to earning nearly $3,000 a month may not seem like a lot to some, but for me, it's monumental," she explains.

Another client, Claudia, set aside $6,000 into investment. Today, that money has enabled her to earn income through eight accounts in different stocks, and two in crypto.

"I entered during a market dip and followed Finanzo's advice closely," she adds. *"In just four months, some investments doubled. I set up automated transfers to invest as soon as I'm paid. I monitor the markets daily—not with panic, but with awareness. I'm fascinated by how society is influenced through finance."*

A year-end gratitude ritual

If you're feeling discouraged or behind financially, take 15 minutes this week to try this exercise:
- List five financial decisions you made this year that you're proud of. They don't have to be big.
- Write down three things you learned about money in the past 12 months.
- Name one person (including yourself!) who helped you grow financially.
- Set an intention for how you want to feel about your money in 2026.

This simple act of reflection turns the page emotionally and energetically—so you can enter the new year from a place of strength, not shame.

Gratitude as financial Strategy

At Finanzo, we believe that financial education must be emotional, not just informational. Gratitude isn't a distraction from strategy; it *is* the foundation of one. When you can acknowledge your own progress, no matter how small, you build the confidence needed to take the next step.

Connect With Maria

www.finanzo.ca/home-en
www.facebook.com/finanzo.ca
www.instagram.com/finanzo.ca
www.tiktok.com/@finanzo.ca
www.youtube.com/@finanzo.ca.
www.linkedin.com/company/finanzo-ca

Becoming An Unstoppable Woman Magazine

YOUR ULTIMATE STRATEGIC TOOL:
HOW TO PHYSIOLOGICALLY OUTPERFORM CRISIS

By **Diana Mirs**

As a digital nomad, I was completely exhausted. Stranded on the road, my foreign bank card got blocked, and I felt lost, super stressed, hopeless, and deeply lonely. My system had failed. I knew the high-octane stress made my brain work in panic mode, not peak performance. I was guaranteed to make mistakes, not clear choices.

But as a Mind-Body Connection coach, I had a specific tool: embodied gratitude. Implementing just five minutes of this practice a couple of times a day helped me instantly shift my inner state. Clarity was restored. It allowed me to make a purposeful decision that reignited my resilience and ensured my future unfolded perfectly.

The crippling overwhelm I felt during that crisis wasn't a temporary fatigue. It was a clear stress response of my body and mind. When motivated women face pressure, the whole system is flooded with cortisol, keeping the brain in panic. It becomes impossible to act as your best self or make sharp decisions when your ancient fight-or-flight mechanism is on.

The key to accessing your peak performance lies in embodied gratitude – a physiological interrupt, the ultimate mind-body connection strategy.

This is far more than positive thinking. Embodied gratitude is the intentional, tangible act of translating safety to the nervous system. By consciously shifting your internal state and focusing on somatic sensations of appreciation, you stimulate the vagus nerve, hitting the *"reset"* button on your entire system.

This is the source of our true resilience. Gratitude activates the prefrontal cortex, the brain's command center for executive function. This enhances optimal clarity, leads to laser focus, and enables the ability to make sharper, less reactive decisions – even under extreme pressure. This simple shift transforms your well-being into an ultimate business tool, ensuring sustained peak performance.

The best part is that embodied gratitude is an accessible tool that requires only two minutes. By deploying these strategic micro-habits, you actively train your nervous system to choose calm over crisis, building a sustainable foundation for unstoppable growth and emotional agility.

1. The 90-Second Vagal Prime

This is the core mind-body connection technique. Immediately upon waking, before a high-pressure meeting, or whenever you feel overwhelmed, pause. Don't just think gratitude – focus on the physical sensations of appreciation (a warmth in your chest, a lightness in your breath, or the stability of your feet). Breathe slowly and intentionally into that feeling, physically experiencing it for 90 seconds. This somatic focus instantly promotes a physiological system reset.

2. The Grounded Re-entry

Immediately following your prime, bypass distractions like your phone. Use your restored optimal clarity to intentionally connect with your immediate surroundings. Notice the scent of your coffee, the light through the window, or the texture of your clothing. This sensory exercise anchors the new feeling of calm directly to your environment, ensuring your brain engages with the world from a place of laser focus and less reactive intention. Consistency is your secret weapon. Let this intentional practice become your resilience muscle, ensuring you fuel your growth and transform pressure into performance daily.

This is the physiological blueprint for thriving. When you regularly practice embodied gratitude, you move past the cycle of reactive survival, being able to curb the crippling effects of cortisol and overwhelm. That is how you become a woman who maintains optimal clarity under fire, makes sharper decisions with unwavering focus, and commands sustained peak performance regardless of external chaos.

You are not just surviving, you are growing and glowing. Harness this intentional practice daily, and fully step into your identity as the resilient, unstoppable woman you are meant to be.

Connect With Diana

www.payhip.com/DianaMirs
www.instagram.com/diana_mirs
www.insighttimer.com/diana_mirs
www.youtube.com/@DailyMindfulnessWithDianaMirs
www.youtube.com/@DailyMeditationsWithDianaMirs
www.linkedin.com/in/diana-mirs

Clearlight®

Infrared Saunas and Wellness Solutions

Discover premium infrared saunas tailored to your needs. Explore various models and sizes.

START YOUR WELLNESS JOURNEY TODAY.

INFRAREDSAUNA.COM

DEBBIE SU:
SHOOTING FOR HER DREAMS

By **Nana Nadal**

Debbie Su grew up in a provincial city in Mindanao, the southern part of the Philippines. These days, one can find her in Los Angeles, establishing herself in the film industry. The 28-year-old is a producer and director at MasterCrash, a learning platform created by David Zucker, who is regarded as one of the most influential forces in spoof comedy. She also lends her filmmaking talents to music artists, restaurants, and cafes.

As far as Debbie can remember, movies have always inspired her. At nine years old, after seeing *"Letters from Iwo Jima"* and *"Flags of Our Fathers,"* she discovered the power of shaping perspective through films. And through the behind-the-scenes footage of *"The Lord of the Rings"* trilogy, she learned how it takes many teams to bring a story to life. From there, she set her sights on crafting her own films and joining the film industry.

While her path was evident early on, it came with obstacles. Her parents, while supportive, encouraged her to learn a more practical profession, so she put aside her passions to follow their wishes. She passed the entrance exams to the prestigious Ateneo de Manila University where she took up Information Design. She was awarded a 75% scholarship, which she maintained throughout her studies. *"As a scholar, I had to do service hours so I was juggling that with classes, homework, extra-curricular activities, and traveling through standstill traffic. My allowance for the week was a sixth of what my classmates had. I would sometimes join my friends when they would eat out, but I wouldn't buy anything,"* she relates. *"But that experience made me a fighter. And I'm grateful that my parents looked out for my education despite the difficulties."*

After graduating in 2018, she spent the next couple of years freelancing. When the pandemic hit, she landed a remote job as a graphic designer. She was quickly promoted to manager and was able to save money to finally work towards her true aspirations. *"Hollywood was the dream. I grew up with a lot of movies and shows that originated in Los Angeles, so it was a clear choice to go there to learn from the greats,"* she says.

Taking up Cinema Production at Los Angeles Community College, she found herself playing catch-up. But what she lacked in experience, she made up for with hard work, and her talent soon became apparent to her teachers and peers. This opened doors for her, and through the school she earned a grant from the Golden Globe Foundation for her film *"RIP in Peace,"*

which is currently on its festival run and has already received some recognition. It was also through the school that she had the chance to meet writer/director David Zucker and within months, become a producer and director on his MasterCrash course on spoof comedy.

Through her journey, she has met people who align with her level of standards and continue to collaborate with her. *"I feel like every time I was passionate about doing a project, I didn't really have a safety net yet I kept finding a community that held me up."* Against all odds, she kept the faith that everything was going to work out. *"This is getting into the spiritual side of things but I always felt like I was called to do this, to the point that I feel like all these struggles in this journey is like a memory. It's like just me reading the story of how I got there and not so much wondering if I'm going to get there,"* she concludes.

Connect With Debbie

www.debisu.com
www.instagram.com/debisufilm

Becoming An Unstoppable Woman Magazine

Becoming An Unstoppable Woman Magazine

December 2025

START 2026 WITH GRATITUDE, LEAVE THE RESOLUTIONS BEHIND IN 2025

By **Pamela Martorana, LPC**

It's closing in at that time of year- when we all start thinking about the new year ahead. The glorious new year, filled with hope and endless possibilities. A new year symbolizes fresh starts, new beginnings, a redo in life.

But what do most people do with this opportunity? They show up with resolutions--yes, dreaded New Year's resolutions. Many times, they are the same ones from years gone by, wash, rinse, repeat. We commit ourselves to losing weight, eating better, exercising more.

Do people actually maintain their resolutions and reach their goals? According to a 2024 Forbes Health/One Poll survey the average resolution lasts just 3.74 months. Longer than I thought they would last! Only 8% of respondents reported sticking with their goals for one month, 22% lasted two months, 22% lasted three months and 13% lasted four months.

So, what if you started 2026 differently? What if you rang in the New Year with gratitude?

New Year's resolutions tend to focus on things we want to change or improve --our perceived flaws. When we focus on what we don't like or want to change about ourselves, we can end up feeling judged and *"less than"* in compared to the next person. But shifting our focus to gratitude puts the abundance and the blessings already in our life in the spotlight. Sometimes when people hear the word gratitude they focus on the larger picture, *"I am grateful for my family, my job etc."* Get granular with your gratitude, be grateful for your ability to hear, see, smell, taste and touch, some people can't. Be grateful for the being alive, breathing, being able to walk down the street and feel safe.

Gratitude helps us recognize what we have in our life and not what we lack. Focusing on appreciation of what we already have in our lives is a much gentler and kinder form of motivation. According to the law of attraction, when we use our energy to focus on the abundance already present in our lives, we will attract more of it.

Of course, many of us will fall prey to making those dreaded resolutions- and that's okay. I am suggesting you integrate gratitude into them and create more balanced and compassionate approach. Gratitude is a positive emotion connected to appreciating and celebrating what is good in our life. Imagine creating new year's resolutions with a dash of gratitude and a sprinkle of celebration.

For example, instead of saying:
"I walk 10,000 steps every day"

Try reframing with gratitude:
"I am grateful for my legs that carry me and help me take a walk each day. I commit to walking between 8,000 and 10,000 steps daily, listening to my body and when it needs rest."

It is the same resolution --but now it honors and acknowledges the work of your body and not seeing it as a failure on days when we do not walk 10,000 steps.

Thinking and creating new year's resolutions through the lends of gratitude invites us to take pause and be gentler with ourselves. Taking pause helps us to remember parts of our lives and ourselves that we may take for granted.

And remember, --we do not need the stroke of midnight on December 31, 2025, or any year, to give us permission to start over. As long as we are breathing, we can start over, try again, to begin anew each and every day.

That in itself, is something to be eternally grateful for in life

Connect With Pamela

Instagram: #martoranapamela
Facebook: Pamela Martorana

Becoming An Unstoppable Woman Magazine

one word to bee better.

PETER BRADFORD & LYNETTE SHARP

THE WOMEN BEHIND MY WORDS:
HOW GRANDMOTHER'S WISDOM AND DAUGHTER'S FUTURE SHAPED THE BEEBETTER MOVEMENT

By **Peter Bradford**

When people ask about the inspiration behind my BeeBetter Movement, they're often surprised when I mention the two most influential women in my life: my grandmother and my daughter Emma.

Grandmother's Gift of Independence

Since childhood, my grandmother was my unconditional supporter. When most adults might laugh at a child's dream of buying a house, she reassured me I could achieve it when older and followed through with practical lessons on money management when I began working at 14.

My first taste of independence came when I moved out of my parents' house and stayed with her. Instead of imposing rules, she gave me room to figure out life as an adult.

Later, with her guidance and financial contribution, I purchased my first home, fulfilling the promise she'd made years earlier. She established the foundation of my financial knowledge, preparing me for success while showering me with hugs and kisses.

Beyond financial wisdom, my grandparents' home was my childhood sanctuary. Fifty acres of woodland with a pond became the setting for countless adventures. My grandfather and I became an inseparable duo during these weekend visits where I learned to appreciate nature's wonders from bird watching to making maple syrup.

These experiences taught me that meaningful connections and shared experiences far outweigh material possessions: a cornerstone of the BeeBetter philosophy.

Emma: The Future of BeeBetter

In my forties, this lesson crystallized as I realized, "*I'd rather spend quality time with my daughter, Emma, than spend money on material things.*" This shift wasn't about depriving ourselves, but recognizing that memories far outlive material possessions.

Emma and I have developed our own traditions, like our Sunday breakfast ritual where we go out for breakfast every Sunday to talk and check in with each other. These moments have become sacred spaces for authentic connection.

While many parents hope their children will follow directly in their footsteps, I've taken a different approach. I don't want Emma to be exactly like me. I want her to take from the best parts of me and build on them. Rather than continuing our exact traditions, I'd prefer she does something more specific to her children's needs in a way that immortalizes her in their memory as a fantastic parent.

It's been remarkable to witness how much it has inspired my daughter, Emma, to realize how limitless she is and how she consistently allows positivity to triumph in her life. Seeing her embrace these principles reassures me that the BeeBetter Movement transcends generations.

From Personal to Universal

The transformation of one woman, Maya, exemplifies how powerful the BeeBetter approach can be. After adopting positive language, replacing "*I'm fine*" with "*I'm awesome,*" Maya's entire outlook shifted. When restructuring hit her workplace, instead of feeling anxious, Maya saw it as an opportunity and successfully secured a leadership position.

Like my grandmother did for me and as I hope to do for Emma, the BeeBetter Movement invites readers to discover their unique "*buzzword*" and realize potential to be great and live it daily.

Remember, being positive isn't about what you have but who you choose to be. It's the commitment to always look on the brighter side of things and strive to be better every day, irrespective of what you own or are going through.

What word will you choose today to honor the women who shaped you and inspire those who will follow?

Connect With Peter

www.beebettermovement.com
www.instagram.com/beebettermovement
www.youtube.com/@beebettermovement

FROM GARDEN TO GLOBAL IMPACT:
CIARA'S JOURNEY AS A FEMALE LEADER

By **Ciara Byrne**
Co-founder & CEO of Green Our Planet

I co-founded Green Our Planet with my partner, Kim MacQuarrie, in 2013 — but this work has lived in me since childhood. I grew up in a working-class neighborhood in Dublin in the 1980s. I struggled with anxiety and didn't have the words to express that. But I knew one thing: when I was outside in the garden helping my parents grow potatoes, or walking the misty Dublin coastline, I felt calm. I felt alive. I felt connected to something larger than myself. Nature, very simply, made me whole.

I've always believed that the power of nature can do the same for every human being — if we're given the chance. Yet today, many children grow up without gardens, without access to nature. A simple experience like pulling a potato from the earth — which expanded my world — is missing from so many childhoods. That understanding planted the first seed of Green Our Planet.

I came to the U.S. in my early twenties, wide-eyed and determined to contribute. While friends pursued corporate careers, I joined the New York Public Interest Research Group, knocking on doors to talk about whales and pollution. Even then, my instinct was to protect the planet and engage people in that mission. Later, I built a film production company in New York, creating documentaries and series for National Geographic, the BBC, PBS, and Discovery. I had achieved the American Dream — but not my dream. I still felt called to tell a deeper story: one about our connection to the Earth and to each other.

That calling became undeniable in Kenya, in the backyard of Dr. Richard Leakey, as Kim and I sat overlooking the Rift Valley discussing the Sixth Extinction. Dr. Leakey said something that changed my life:

"If people can fall in love with the Earth, they'll want to protect it."

That idea became our north star. At Green Our Planet, we help students fall in love with the planet by growing food — in school gardens and through hydroponics systems in classrooms. We train teachers to use gardens as living STEM labs where lessons come alive through soil, light, roots, and leaves. Math, science, engineering, nutrition, teamwork, and entrepreneurship suddenly become real ways to become hands-on in a joyful way. We focus especially on students living in food deserts and communities without access to green space, helping them see food not as scarcity but as possibility — something they can grow, share, and take pride in.

What began with one school garden in Las Vegas has grown into the largest school garden and hydroponics program in the United States. Today we serve more than 1,300 schools across 44 states, reaching over 500,000 students — and by 2033, we plan to reach 10,000 communities and 5 million young people.

Our programs don't just grow vegetables — they grow confidence, curiosity, resilience, and hope. They grow future chefs, farmers, scientists, engineers, and entrepreneurs. And maybe most importantly, they grow young people who understand that life on Earth is precious, rare, and worth protecting.

I am constantly inspired by the teachers who make this work real. Many email us long after the school day ends — researching lessons, troubleshooting hydroponics systems, dreaming up farmers markets for their students. Their dedication wakes me up every morning with gratitude and purpose. The truth is, I began this journey searching for belonging and connection. What I found is that when you give children a chance to connect with the Earth — to put their hands in soil, to grow something living — they begin to feel connected to themselves, to each other, and to their future.

And that is how we grow a generation ready to heal the world, one seed — and one child — at a time.

Connect With Ciara

www.GreenOurPlanet.org
Instagram: @GreenOurPlanet
X: @GreenOurPlanet2
Facebook: Green Our Planet
LinkedIn: Green Our Planet

EMPOWERHER CONTENT DAY

ONE STADIUM. 40,000 WOMEN. INFINITE IMPACT

02 | 22 | 2026

A NEW CHAPTER BEGINS

FENIX TV

IS NOW ON YOUTUBE

TUNE IN FOR THE SAME INSPIRING CONTENT YOU LOVE, NOW ON A GLOBAL STAGE.

THE MISSING LINK TO FEELING BETTER:

Understanding the Vagus Nerve & the Gut-Brain Connection

By **Sheena L. Smith**

If you've been feeling *"off"* lately — low energy, anxious, bloated, foggy, overwhelmed, or just not like yourself — you're not alone. Many women experience these shifts and assume it's just stress, hormones, or getting older and blame is on aging. But more and more research is pointing toward a surprising root cause: a communication breakdown in the vagus nerve and the gut–brain axis.

This isn't just science jargon. It's the beautiful built-in system God gave us to regulate mood, digestion, inflammation, immunity, and even how safe we feel in our own bodies. When the vagus nerve becomes sluggish or the gut gets out of balance, everything else starts to wobble.

Let's unpack it in simple, practical, "this actually makes sense" language — and explore small, gentle things you can do each day to feel more vibrant, grounded, and fully alive again.

What Is the Vagus Nerve & Why Does It Matter?

Your vagus nerve is the longest cranial nerve in your body. It runs from your brainstem, down your neck, through the chest, and into your gut — touching your heart, lungs, digestive organs, and more. Think of it as your internal communication cable.

When it's working well, it sends calming signals that help you digest food, regulate your heartbeat, balance emotions, and shift out of *"fight-or-flight"* into safety and ease.

When it's underactive or stressed, you may experience:
- Anxiety or overstimulation
- Digestive issues (bloating, constipation, IBS-type symptoms)
- Feeling wired yet tired
- Low resilience to stress
- Sleep disruptions
- Brain fog
- Increased inflammation
- Low mood or irritability

A sluggish vagus nerve doesn't scream for attention — it whispers. But those whispers add up. Believe me I know through my own health issues.

Your gut brain -axis is like your second operating system. More than 90% of the vagus nerve's signals travel from the gut to the brain, not the other way around.

Your gut microbiome — the trillions of tiny organisms living in your digestive system — produces neurotransmitters like serotonin, dopamine, and GABA. These chemicals influence your mood, appetite, sleep, energy, and emotional wellbeing.

If your gut is unbalanced, inflamed, or stressed? Your brain feels it.

If your brain is overwhelmed, anxious, or exhausted? Your gut feels it.

This is the gut–brain axis, and the vagus nerve is the messenger connecting the two.

This is why improving digestion, calming inflammation, and supporting the microbiome can have such a profound effect on mood and overall wellbeing.

Proper Nutrition Plays a Big Role

You don't have to overhaul your entire diet to support better vagus nerve tone and gut health. Small daily choices shift the terrain dramatically.

Foods That Support Gut–Brain Wellness

1. Fermented foods
– sauerkraut, kimchi, kefir, yogurt, kombucha
Support beneficial bacteria and help digestion.
2. Polyphenol-rich foods
– blueberries, cranberries, green tea, dark chocolate, olives
Reduce inflammation and feed good gut microbes.
3. Omega-3 fatty acids
– salmon, sardines, walnuts, chia and flaxseed
Support brain health and calm the nervous system.
4. Prebiotic fibres
– asparagus, onions, garlic, bananas, oats
These feed the gut microbiome — like fertilizer for your inner garden.
5. Magnesium-rich foods
– leafy greens, pumpkin seeds, almonds, avocados
Magnesium helps regulate stress, sleep, and nerve relaxation.

Foods to Reduce if You Want Calmer Signals

- Ultra-processed foods
- Artificial sweeteners
- High-sugar snacks
- Excess caffeine
- Alcohol
- Seed oils

You don't have to eliminate anything forever — just reduce what inflames the system so your gut and vagus nerve can function better.

Simple, Daily Vagus Nerve Toning Ideas

These gentle practices that signal safety to your nervous system and strengthen vagal tone over time.

1. Deep, slow breathing
Try 4 seconds in, 6 seconds out. Longer exhales activate your vagus nerve.
2. Cold exposure
Splash cold water on your face or end your shower with 20–30 seconds of cold.
3. Humming or singing
The vibration stimulates the vagus nerve near the vocal cords.
4. Gargling
Surprisingly effective for stimulating the nerve pathways in the throat.
5. Gentle movement
Walking, yoga, stretching — anything that promotes circulation and calm.
6. Laughter
Real, belly laughter (your specialty!) actually increases vagal tone.
7. Mindfulness or prayer
Quieting the mind enhances parasympathetic activity.

None of these require extra time — they simply invite the body back into balance.

A Natural Option That Acts Like a Vagus Nerve *"Activator"*

Many people are now discovering that a certain plant-based ingredient can help nudge the vagus nerve into healthy signaling again. Some extracts work by stimulating the sensory pathways near the mouth and throat — gently activating the nerve and helping the gut–brain axis communicate more clearly.

It's not a magic pill, and it's definitely not a pharmaceutical shortcut.

But for many women, especially over 40, this kind of natural nervous-system support becomes the missing puzzle piece alongside good food, movement, and stress reduction.

If you've been curious about natural solutions that support vagus nerve tone, calm inflammation, or help rebalance digestion and mood — there are options worth exploring.

If this topic resonates and you want:
- foods that boost vagus nerve tone
- lifestyle habits that calm the gut–brain axis
- a list of natural plant ingredients that support this system
- plus a simple daily plan you can start right away

I created a free resource that pulls it all together in one place.

Just let me know and I'll send it your way — no pressure, no commitment, just helpful information so you can make the best choices for your health and happiness.

Connect With Sheena

www.sheenalsmith.com
Facebook: sheenazzy2

HELP, MY BABY WON'T STOP CRYING!

A SIMPLE GUIDE FOR NEW PARENTS

NOW AVAILABLE ON
amazon

Becoming An Unstoppable Woman Magazine

THE PSYCHOLOGY OF KINDNESS AND BOUNDARIES:
WHY LIMITS ARE LOVING

By **Melissa Swonger**
Ph.D. Candidate, M.A. | Founder, The Sage Hill Project

We often mistake kindness for constant availability—saying yes, keeping the peace, and stretching ourselves too thin. But that's not kindness. That's depletion disguised as love.

True kindness is strength with restraint, compassion with boundaries. It's grounded, discerning, and sustainable **only when it has boundaries**.

Both clinical psychology and faith teach the same truth: loving yourself is the precursor to loving others well. Healthy boundaries don't limit love; they protect it.

Boundaries are clarity. They define where generosity ends and self-abandonment begins. When we zoom out and take a 30,000-foot view, we can make a neutral observation without judgment about ways we may give in to co-dependent tendencies or people-pleasing behaviors, and then we're empowered to change.

This holiday season, take an inventory. Identify areas that steal peace and joy. Then, create a solid plan with mental rehearsals, which establish viable brain pathways as alternative behaviors to default practices.

1. Awareness: The Foundation of Boundaries

Cognitive Behavioral Therapy (CBT) teaches that growth begins with awareness—you can't change what you can't name.

Boundaries start by noticing where your peace begins to fray. Ask:
- What consistently leaves me drained?
- What restores me?
- When do I feel resentment?

Resentment often signals that a boundary has been crossed or never communicated. This realization may lead to a boundary that needs to emerge.

Clarify your values—faith, rest, honesty, connection—and let them guide what you protect.

Awareness shifts boundaries from guilt to alignment. You're not rejecting others; you're honoring what has been entrusted to you.

"You can't tame what you can't name."

2. Communication: Speak the Truth in Love

Dialectical Behavior Therapy (DBT) emphasizes *interpersonal effectiveness*: combining assertiveness with empathy.

Healthy boundaries sound clear but compassionate. They acknowledge that two things can be true simultaneously when we use the word *'and.'*

Try:
- *"I love you, and I can't talk about that tonight."*
- *"I value this time, and I need to leave by nine."*

Boundaries are strongest when delivered calmly and early. You don't need to overexplain; consistency with action communicates far more than defense.

"Kindness without boundaries is chaos. Boundaries without kindness are cruelty. Strength is using both."

When you communicate boundaries with clarity and care, you create safety—both for yourself and for others.

3. Protection: Guarding What's Sacred

Family Systems Theory teaches differentiation—knowing where you end and others begin.

You are responsible **to** others, not **for** them.

Many of us grew up equating love with rescuing, fixing, or pleasing everyone. But when you chronically take responsibility for others' emotions, you lose sight of your own.

Boundaries are not selfish; they are a form of stewardship. They protect your purpose and peace, so you can give from an overflow, not a state of depletion.

During the holidays, we can draw on a biblical example. Even Jesus withdrew from the crowds to pray. He modeled engagement and rest—boundaries that made His ministry sustainable.

You can't pour living water from an empty well. Protect the source.

4. Action: Boundaries Require Follow-Through

Behavioral psychology reminds us that people learn from actions, not explanations.

A boundary that's stated but not upheld is a suggestion. A boundary followed through becomes truth. Boundaries upheld inconsistently cause confusion.

If someone crosses a line, restate the limit kindly and follow through:
- *"I'll step away until we can talk respectfully."*
- *"That doesn't work for me right now."*

Avoid long justifications—steady repetition builds trust. When we accuse others in ways that trigger their brain to defend, justify, or otherwise engage negatively, change is no longer possible. Instead, simply follow through on your boundary with action and then reach out amicably another time. If the boundary is still being violated, repeat the action to guard your safety. Emphasize the desire to connect from a healthy space.

When we uphold boundaries calmly, we teach others how to interact safely and respectfully. Behaviorally consistent boundaries turn chaos into clarity.

5. Healing: Rewiring Attachment Through Boundaries

Attachment research shows that many of us learned early that love required self-abandonment or silence.

Healthy limits retrain the nervous system to believe: *I can be connected and still be safe.*

Each time you honor your boundary, you rewire your brain to associate love with peace, not anxiety.

Spiritually, boundaries mirror divine order. Creation itself was formed by separation—light from darkness, sea from sky, work from rest. Boundaries don't hinder love; they reveal its shape and allow all parts of the same team to work both independently and together in a functional manner.

"Boundaries are the bones of healthy connection—unseen but holding everything upright."

6. Compassion: The Heart of Boundaries

Mindfulness-based therapy reminds us that self-compassion is essential for sustaining emotional health.

When guilt surfaces after saying *"no,"* pause and ask: *Is this guilt or a sign of growth?*

Growth feels uncomfortable because it challenges old programming that equated sacrifice with virtue. Codependent tendencies can be triggered when we feel we have to make another feel ok to be ok ourselves.

Remind yourself: *It's okay to disappoint others to remain aligned with peace. You are not responsible for how someone else feels or responds.*

Rest after emotionally heavy interactions. Recovery is part of responsibility.

Kindness toward yourself builds resilience; it's a psychological and spiritual act of repair. One of the most important boundaries is the self-talk in our brains. Celebrate when you uphold your boundaries.

7. This Holiday, Lead with Peace

Boundaries are a form of leadership — self-leadership.

They help you cultivate the internal culture of your own heart, allowing you to bring calm into chaotic environments.

So this year, as you gather around tables filled with both laughter and complexity, remember:
You don't have to attend every argument you're invited to.
You don't have to please everyone to honor God.
You can choose peace and still be kind.

Final Thought

Boundaries are not the opposite of kindness; they are kindness with direction.

They turn chaos into clarity and compassion into sustainability.

When you lead yourself with calm conviction, you model what healthy love looks like—firm, gentle, and free.

Say no when your spirit says no.
Rest without apology.
Speak truth with tenderness.
That's not selfishness. That's stewardship.

Because **Radical Kindness** isn't about pleasing everyone—it's about protecting what's sacred so that love can last.

"Boundaries don't keep love out. They enable integrated, healthy love."

Connect With Melissa

www.thesagehillproject.com
www.linkedin.com/in/melissa-swonger-50b68a37a
www.facebook.com/melissa.j.swonger
www.instagram.com/melissa_swonger

LAUNCH A MONETIZABLE
TOP 1% PODCAST IN 1 HOUR

Finally create a podcast blueprint that builds trust, attracts leads, and turns your mic into money, without content overwhelm or tech spirals.

Scale your lead-generating podcast in just 60 minutes using a proven blueprint trusted by a Top 1% host. Whether you're starting fresh or stuck in strategy spirals, you'll walk away clear, confident, and ready to be heard by the people who need your help most.

🎙 As proven on The Affluent CEO Show
Top 1% ranked podcast with over **67.7K downloads in the last 90 days** and **30.3K in the last 30 days alone**—proven strategies that attract, convert, and scale.

Here's what you get inside:

✔ A soul-aligned 3-part plan to position your podcast, map magnetic content, and connect episodes directly to your offers
✔ A plug-and-play episode planner so you know exactly what to say and when
✔ Your own custom-trained GPT to generate aligned content + promos on demand
✔ A monetization map that links your message to money–with heart-led integrity
✔ A zero-overwhelm tech checklist so you can launch without spiraling or stalling

🎙Launch your monetisable Top 1% podcast in just 60 minutes, complete with custom tools, content generator, and ready to go strategy.

👉 Check the link for more →
yulianafrancie.com/micdrop

Your voice creates an everlasting legacy. Create a platform that supports your growth while building wealth with ease.

WITHOUT YOUR HEALTH, WHAT DO YOU HAVE?

By **Lida Johnson**

We live in a world where success is often measured by the titles we hold, the homes we buy, the vacations we post, and the goals we check off. But underneath all of that, one truth remains constant: without your health, what do you really have?

My name is Lida, and I'm a Health and Wellness Strategist. I help people reclaim their health and energy by blending simple, sustainable habits into their busy, everyday lives — so they can feel strong, confident, and free to chase their biggest dreams.

Health is the foundation that supports everything — your relationships, dreams, energy, and joy. Yet too often, we take it for granted, treating it like something we'll *"get to"* when life slows down. But your health doesn't wait. It speaks to you every day — through your energy, sleep, mood, and motivation. The question is: are you listening?

Health Is a Journey, Not a Destination

Health isn't a finish line - it's a lifelong journey. A relationship with your body, mind, and spirit that evolves as you do. There will be seasons of strength and confidence, and seasons of struggle. But progress, not perfection, is the goal.

The key to sustainable wellness is not about overhauling your life overnight; it lies in the small, intentional choices made consistently. Go for that walk. Choose real, nourishing food. Set boundaries. Give yourself grace. Each decision is a small act of self-respect that compounds over time.

Health Is Complex — and Beautifully So

Health is far more than what you eat or how you move. According to the World Health Organization, health is *"a state of complete physical, mental, and social well-being, and not merely the absence of disease or infirmity."*

When one area is neglected, the others start to wobble. Health is like a puzzle – all the interconnected pieces create the true picture. True wellness requires awareness, balance, and compassion, not punishment or perfectionism.

Freedom Is a Choice

I often hear, *"I want the freedom to eat, drink, and do whatever I want…"* But freedom doesn't happen by accident. Freedom is a choice — to prioritize healthy habits over unhealthy ones, to take action even when it's uncomfortable, to believe that you are worth it. Every positive choice brings you closer to the freedom to live the life you dream of.

The Heart of the Journey: Self-Love

The hardest part of health is learning to love yourself enough to stay consistent — through the wins and the slip-ups. Self-hate whispers that you'll never change. Self-love says, *"You're worth it."* Even if you don't believe it, I do.

When you focus on making better choices each day, everything else starts to fall into place naturally. Food becomes fuel, movement becomes a celebration, and rest becomes rejuvenation. You stop chasing *"perfect"* and start building a life that is uniquely yours - strong, balanced, and free.

A Reminder

Your body is your lifelong home. Your mind shapes your reality. Your spirit gives your life meaning. When you nurture all of you, you gain the strength, freedom, and confidence to chase your biggest dreams — and enjoy and thrive in them.

True health is about presence — showing up for yourself, again and again, no matter how many times you've fallen off track.

If you're ready to take back your health and your freedom, I can help. Through 1:1 coaching or by joining my group 8-Week Healthy Jumpstart Program, your head-to-toe health journey will begin.

Because when you feel healthy, you feel free — and that's when you can chase your dreams with full force and an open heart.

Connect With Lida

www.headtotoecoaching.com
www.instagram.com/lidaheadtotoe
www.linkedin.com/in/headtotoecoaching
www.facebook.com/LidaLJohnson

Becoming An Unstoppable Woman Magazine

THE MASK OF "I'M FINE":
LETTING GOD HEAL THE HIDDEN HURT

December 2025

By **Elizabeth Meigs**
Transformational Coach & Messenger of God's Miracle Power™

I used to think strength meant keeping it all together — smiling when I wanted to cry, saying *"I'm fine"* while my heart was breaking. For years, that mask was my armor, I thought it was protecting me from judgment yet imprisoning me in silence.

Maybe you know that mask too. You show up for everyone else, hold it together at work, and whisper to yourself, Just get through the day. But pretending doesn't heal you; it only buries the pain deeper. And God can't heal what we keep hiding — not because He can't see it, but because He won't force His way in.

I learned that truth the hard way. After trauma turned my world upside down, I convinced everyone I was okay. Outwardly, I looked strong; inwardly, I was unraveling. It wasn't until I broke down before God that real healing began.

Psalm 34:18 promises, *"The Lord is close to the brokenhearted and saves those who are crushed in spirit."* When I finally brought my crushed spirit to Him — anger, grief, fear, and all — He didn't shame me. He surrounded me with peace. I discovered that being seen by God isn't scary; it's safe.

From a neuroscience perspective, that moment of honesty changed more than my emotions. Studies show that when we suppress feelings, the brain treats them as danger signals, keeping the body in fight-or-flight mode. But when we name what we feel — even in prayer — the brain releases calming chemicals like oxytocin, the *"connection hormone."* Vulnerability literally rewires the mind toward safety and connection.

That's why honesty is holy ground. Every time you tell God the truth, you quiet the storm inside your nervous system. You make room for grace to rewrite your story.

If you've been living behind your own version of *"I'm fine,"* maybe it's time to set the mask down. You don't have to have the perfect words; you just have to show up. Start with this simple prayer:
"Father, You see the parts of me I've been hiding. I'm tired of pretending I'm okay. Meet me here. Show me what You want to heal."

Then take five minutes to journal one emotion you've been avoiding. Don't edit it — just write. Notice what happens inside your body as you invite God into that space. Maybe your shoulders drop, your breathing slows, or your heart feels lighter. That's the beginning of healing.

Strength isn't pretending you're fine; it's having the courage to be real. God can't heal what we hide, but He can redeem anything we reveal. When we say, *"Here I am, Lord — broken but willing,"* He meets us right there.

So today, take off the mask. Let Him see you, love you, and lead you back to peace. Because the same God who healed me is ready to heal the hidden hurts in you too.

To hear the full story and learn practical ways to break free from burnout and emotional exhaustion, listen to my podcast Untrapped: Healing the Invisible Wounds to Living Your Dreams on Apple Podcasts, Spotify, or your favorite platform.

Visit ElizabethInspires.com for free resources, including my Daily Affirmations Text Series and the Pathway to PEACE Method™ — faith-based tools to help you rise, reframe, and reconnect with the life God designed for you.

Because healing begins with honesty, and wholeness begins when you stop hiding and let God in.

Connect With Elizabeth

www.elizabethinspires.com
www.elizabethinspires.com/podcast-1
www.instagram.com/elizabethmeigsinspires
www.linkedin.com/in/elizabethinspires
www.youtube.com/@elizabethinspires

SHOP NOW

GRAB YOUR COPY NOW

Possibility to Prosperity is an inspiring anthology featuring bold, visionary women who turned their greatest struggles into triumphs. Through honest and powerful stories, these women reveal how pain can become purpose, fear can become fuel, and setbacks can spark success. From heartbreak and burnout to rejection and failure, each chapter offers lessons in resilience, reinvention, and reclaiming one's worth. With courage and determination, these stories illuminate the path from challenge to opportunity, showing that it's never too late to rise, build, and thrive. This book reminds every reader that your struggles can be the gateway to your greatest possibilities.

amazon.com   SHE RISES STUDIOS

Becoming An Unstoppable Woman Magazine

DREAMING INTO THE NEW YEAR:

HOW A DREAM PRACTICE CAN KICKSTART YOUR CREATIVITY AND ENERGIZE YOUR NEW YEAR

By **Bonnie Buckner, PhD**
Author, The Secret Mind: Unlock the Power of Dreams to Transform Your Life

Winter is around the corner, and with it a new year, giving us a moment to reset and create the space for new opportunities.

As a creative dreamwork expert, I find with clients that one of the greatest challenges to creativity is the pressure to get things done. This pressure to produce and complete long to-do lists belongs to the externalization phase of creativity, and is characterized by constant activity. While this is an important aspect of creativity, it comes second to ideation. Ideation is the internal phase which requires unstructured time away from the activity of making. Time when we pause, look inside, and allow our minds to drift... and dream.

The long nights of winter mean more time sleeping which opens us to dreaming. Dreaming is very nexus of our creativity. Not only does dreaming and creative insight share the same neural processing system called the default network, dreaming puts us in strange scenarios with unexpected experiences that elicit new ideas and perspectives.

Catching the new ideas of dreams is as simple as creating a dreaming practice. Whether you already have a robust dream life, or if you don't remember your dreams, by setting up a dreaming practice you will not only begin to remember your dreams more frequently, they will become increasingly elaborate as you begin to interact with them.

A dream practice begins by getting a dream journal – one that you really enjoy and look forward to filling with your ideas. Writing, more than using your phone, will help you to remember your dreams and capture all the unusual aspects that auto correct tends to change. Keep the journal by your bed, with a pen, and when you wake, write down anything and everything you remember, without stopping to ask if it makes sense or not. Lingering in that dreamy half-wake space a bit longer is a juicy creative time, so be sure to also capture any reflections that arise in that space as well.

Pausing is an integral part of renewal. Whether it is about creative projects at work, or the creative project of the individual self, without pausing we begin to repeat old ideas or just run out of inspiration. Dreaming provides a natural pause each night when we can pull ourselves away from output, and enjoy the rich, creative input from the resources of our inner landscape.

Starting a dream practice, as we wind down the current year, can be the perfect time to create this new habit. Choosing to pause and reflect is exactly what the season around us is doing. Putting the intention to capture the new insights waiting to appear sets us up to ring in a very creative new year.

Connect With Bonnie

www.institutefordreamingandimagery.com
www.bonniebuckner.com
www.instagram.com/dreamwithiidi
www.facebook.com/drbonniebuckner
www.instagram.com/bonniebucknerdotcom

A LEGACY OF STRENGTH, FAITH, AND PURPOSE

By **She Rises Studios Editorial Team**

In a world where achievement often overshadows authenticity, Nadia Sheikh stands as a powerful reminder that true success means more when it serves others. With a distinguished career in finance and a life dedicated to service, mentorship, and personal growth, Nadia embodies what it means to lead with both excellence and empathy. Her journey is one of balance, between professional brilliance and heartfelt purpose, between ambition and compassion, and between the drive to achieve and the grace to uplift.

For Nadia, professional excellence has never been just about climbing the ladder or collecting accolades. It is about creating opportunity, fostering inclusion, and building systems that help others succeed. When asked how she balances her demanding career in finance with her deep passion for social impact, she responds with striking clarity: *"It's all about time management. I know how much time in the day I need for my work and how much time commitment is needed."*

That sense of structure did not always come easily. Nadia admits that her journey once included burnout and overextension. *"I will admit it was not always like this. I used to have burnouts. Now I focus on what needs to be worked on and time accordingly. It is also being able to adapt when need be."* Through experience and reflection, she learned that sustainability in leadership comes not from doing more, but from doing what truly matters.

That mindset, grounded in adaptability and self-awareness, defines how she approaches every facet of her life. Beyond finance, Nadia's story is one of endurance and creativity. From writing three anthologies to completing five marathons and climbing the CN Tower, she is a woman who refuses to be confined by limits. *"A lot of these things stem from my childhood in what has been ingrained into me,"* she shares. *"I have a lot of energy in me, so I like to channel it in productive ways. I also like to challenge myself. I am my own competition. I like to see how I can be better than yesterday."*

Her drive is not about outperforming others but about self-evolution. *"I like to improve myself on a daily basis,"* she says. That daily commitment to growth, discipline, and purpose is what fuels her. Every finish line crossed, every book published, and every life touched is a reflection of her belief that progress is the truest form of success.

Even as a child, Nadia displayed the dedication that would later define her leadership. By the age of ten, she was already volunteering, learning early the value of giving back. At fifteen, she earned her black belt in martial arts, an achievement that taught her focus, consistency, and respect. *"As I was coming up, I never thought I was setting a standard for anyone,"* she recalls.

"I was constantly trying to prove to myself that I can do anything and had always tried to be better than I was from the day before."

While her own determination carried her far, Nadia is quick to acknowledge the foundation that shaped her. She credits her parents as a major source of strength and guidance. Their values, love, and example set the tone for the woman she would become. *"My parents played a huge role in my upbringing and in shaping who I am today,"* she shares. Their support created the environment where service, resilience, faith, and hard work became a natural way of life.

Those early experiences, combined with strong family influence, shaped the leader Nadia would become: humble, grounded, and purpose-driven. *"I like to lead by example,"* she says. *"I am not one of those people who can direct people. That's why I could never be a people manager. I was always good at giving back and actually paving a path."*

To Nadia, leadership is not about authority. It is about action. It is about creating impact quietly, consistently, and authentically. Her story illustrates that leadership is not something granted. It is something earned through integrity and example.

Yet even the strongest leaders are shaped by the challenges that test them most. In recent years, Nadia has endured profound personal loss, losing both her husband three years ago and her beloved dog just three weeks ago. *"Sometimes I don't know how I do it,"* she says softly. *"But all I can credit to is Allah. Because of the faith I had in Allah since childhood, faith has helped me to push forward."*

Faith, meditation, and grounding have become the pillars that sustain her. *"Just giving back helps me with purpose,"* she adds. In the face of grief, Nadia has found strength through service, continuing to pour into her community, mentor others, and find beauty in resilience. Her faith in Allah remains the foundation that steadies her in all seasons.

That spiritual grounding flows naturally into her work with grassroots causes and youth mentorship. Having volunteered since childhood, Nadia now uses her experiences to guide young people as they discover their voice and purpose. Her advice to them is simple but profound: *"Never give up when life is hard. Never hold anything in and just speak up because your voice matters."*

Her message to the next generation is one of courage and conviction. *"If there is anything you want to do or achieve in life, just go for it,"* she says. *"It's better to say that you have done it than not to have tried at all. No matter what the outcome is, win or lose, it doesn't matter because at the end of the day you can say, I did it."*

Those words capture the essence of who Nadia Sheikh is, a woman who leads by living boldly, faithfully, and fearlessly. Her life is not defined by the titles she has earned, but by the example she sets: that perseverance is strength, that faith is fuel, and that legacy is built through purpose.

Her story reminds us that leadership does not always roar. Sometimes, it is found in quiet discipline, in service to others, and in the daily choice to keep moving forward, no matter how heavy the day may feel.

As 2025 comes to a close, Nadia continues to embody what it means to lead a life of meaning and motion. She is not just creating success; she is creating significance. Every chapter of her story, from the boardroom to the marathon track, testifies to her belief that when one woman rises, she lifts others with her.

For Nadia Sheikh, life has never been about waiting for permission to lead. It is about leading with purpose, living with faith, honoring the family who shaped her, and leaving a mark that will never fade.

Connect With Nadia

www.threads.com/@sheikhnad2025
www.facebook.com/share/17GPBRseDe
www.linkedin.com/in/nadiasheikh1

GRAB YOUR COPY NOW

She Endures: Perseverance Through Pain is a heartfelt anthology honoring women who have faced life's hardest moments and chosen to rise. Through honest, powerful stories of illness, loss, heartbreak, and healing, this collection reveals how pain can shape strength and purpose. Each chapter offers hope, reminding readers that endurance is not just surviving, but growing through what we overcome. Featuring Hanna Olivas, Adriana Luna Carlos, and 11 inspiring authors, this book is a testament to the resilience of women who refuse to give up.

amazon.com   SHE RISES STUDIOS

GET YOUR COPY NOW

Celebrate the power of women through inspiring stories and insights.

FAITH, FREEDOM & OTHER F WORDS
RHIANNON ANDERSON

THE ABCS OF SELF-LOVE
AMIE RICH

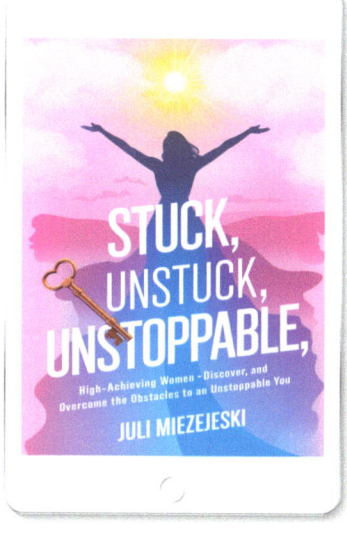

STUCK, UNSTUCK, UNSTOPPABLE
JULIA MIEZEJESKI

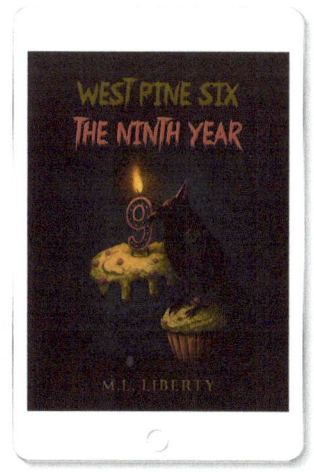

WEST PINE SIX: THE NINTH YEAR
MARIE LAURA LIBERTY

STRETCH & STRETCH JUNIOR
MICHELE KLINE

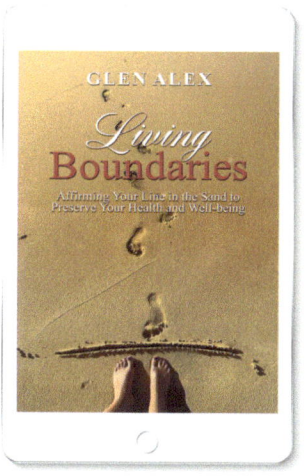

LIVING BOUNDARIES

 SHOP NOW PUBLISHED BY SHE RISES STUDIOS

www.ingramcontent.com/pod-product-compliance
Lightning Source LLC
LaVergne TN
LVHW070438080526
838202LV00035B/2657